Back from the shadows

Mengelberg Mitropoulos Abendroth van Beinum

Discographies compiled by John Hunt

CONTENTS

3 Acknowledgement

4 Introduction

7 Willem Mengelberg

87 Hermann Abendroth

125 Hermann Abendroth: a postcript

127 Dimitri Mitropoulos

228 Dimitri Mitropoulos: interviews

229 Dimitri Mitropoulos: compositions

241 Eduard van Beinum

299 Credits

Published 1997 by John Hunt
Designed by Richard Chlupaty, London
Printed by Short Run Press, Exeter
ISBN 1 9013950 2 2

ACKNOWLEDGEMENT

These publications have been made possible by contributions and advance subscriptions from the following:

Masakasu Abe, Chiba
Richard Ames, New Barnet
Stefano Angeloni, Frasso Sabino
Stathis Arfanis, Athens
Yoshihiro Asada, Osaka
Jack Atkinson, Tasmania
Eduardo Chibas, Caracas
Robert Christoforides, Fordingbridge
F. De Vilder, Bussum
Richard Dennis, Greenhithe
John Derry, Newcastle-upon-Tyne
Hans-Peter Ebner, Milan
Henry Fogel, Chicago
Peter Fu, Hong Kong
Nobuo Fukumoto, Hamamatsu
Peter Fulop, Toronto
James Giles, Sidcup
Jens Golumbus, Hamburg
Jean-Pierre Goossens, Luxembourg
Gordon Grant, Seattle
Johann Gratz, Vienna
Michael Harris, London
Tadashi Hasegawa, Nagoya
Naoya Hirabayashi, Tokyo
Donald Hodgman, Riverside CN
Martin Holland, Sale
Bodo Igesz, New York
Richard Igler, Vienna
Shiro Kawai, Tokyo
Andrew Keener, New Malden
Detlef Kissmann, Solingen
Elisabeth Legge-Schwarzkopf DBE, Zürich
John Mallinson, Hurst Green
Carlo Marinelli, Rome
Finn Moeller Larsen, Virum
Philip Moores, Stafford
Bruce Morrison, Gillingham
W. Moyle, Ombersley
Alan Newcombe, Hamburg
Hugh Palmer, Chelmsford
Jim Parsons, Sutton Coldfield
Laurence Pateman, London
James Pearson, Vienna
Johann Christian Petersen, Hamburg
Tully Potter, Billericay
Patrick Russell, Calstock
Yves Saillard, Mollie-Margot
Neville Sumpter, Northolt
Yoshihiko Suzuki, Tokyo
H.A. Van Dijk, Apeldoorn
Mario Vicentini, Cassano Magnago
Hiromitsu Wada, Chiba
Urs Weber, St Gallen
Nigel Wood, London
G. Wright, Romford

BACK FROM THE SHADOWS

Contrary to all expectations the age of the compact disc has opened up vistas of the gramophone's history and has given new life to vast areas of the classical catalogue which had lain unexposed more or less since the days of shellac. Archives of taped radio broadcasts dating back to the 1930s and 1940s have supplemented the gramophone's official legacy to bring an awareness of musical activity and past traditions over the major part of our century.

Yet in spite of all this a number of important conducting careers from the past continue to languish in relative obscurity, and this almost always for non-musical reasons. The choice of conductors for this volume of discographies aims to rectify the imbalance which mars general appreciation of certain figures.

Political reasons - or more precisely the musician's willingness to let himself become associated with an authoritarian regime - have long been a stumbling block. In the case of Nazi Germany, which was defeated a full half century ago, one must question the motives of those who continue to point the moral finger with an obsessive hatred worthy of any dogged political persuasion.

Opinions about **Willem Mengelberg**'s "politics" - like most performers he probably had none - have tended to restrict appreciation of his art to a limited inner circle of enthusiasts. Mengelberg seems to have been punished for working in German-occupied Holland during World War II more severely than any of the German nationals who were subsequently rehabilitated. Mengelberg was quite simply not rehabiliated, and the recording career as we have it - prewar shellacs and 1930s-1940s radio broadcasts - was not resumed. No matter, for integrity and intensity, an autocratic sovereignty within the framework of an extreme inspirational freedom, shine through the grooves of sessions like the 1927-1932 Columbias, not to mention the earlier Victor recordings with the New York Philharmonic or later Telefunkens. That legendary 1928 New York Heldenleben is not alone in Mengelberg's work in its combination of ultra-fidelity and inspired zeal. It demands to be included in any short list of the Dutchman's top achievements, to which I would add my personal choice of Liszt's Les Préludes, one or other of the Tchaikovsky Pathétiques, Brahms Ein deutsches Requiem (also considered by John Steane in "Choral music on record" to be the most fascinating recording of the work) and one delicious gem: the Turkish March from Beethoven's incidental music to "The Ruins of Athens", where a Beecham-like pointing and swagger make this occasional piece into the sort of record which one can play again and again with never-diminishing enthusiasm.

Hermann Abendroth, the single German in our gallery, was in 1933 dismissed from his Cologne conducting post, which he had held successfully for virtually two decades, for, among other reasons, giving work to too many Jewish musicians. He was entrusted instead with the Leipzig Gewandhaus post vacated by Bruno Walter, and in 1945 chose to remain in the Communist zone of Germany - this was a voluntary choice, for the Berlin Wall did not exist in Abendroth's lifetime. His official recording career was small, although surprisingly it did include Brahms symphonies in London in the early days of electrical recording. However, a veritable storehouse of archive tapes from during and after the war are now being systematically examined and published by the enterprising Tahra label. They burn like a beacon in their manic obsession, totally disregarding gramophone etiquette (huge ritardandi, swaggering minuets and ferocious climaxes are but a few of the characteristics). This is music-making which by its very nature cannot be smooth or consistent but which will set Abendroth alongside Furtwängler and Mengelberg as one of the great musical individualists of the century. As a representative selection from the discography so far I might choose symphonies by Haydn (No 97), Schumann (No 1) and Bruckner (No 7) - but be warned, there is still more of this combustible conducting to be unearthed!

As soon becomes clear when reading William Trotter's recent biography of the Greek conductor **Dimitri Mitropoulos**, this ultra-sensitive musician was, like John Barbirolli before him, an unlikely candidate to take on those hard-bitten individuals who called themselves the New York Philharmonic Symphony Orchestra. Nor did the New York public really thank Mitropoulos for the catholicity of his repertoire. Most of the commercial recordings have languished in comparative obscurity simply because they were carried out just before the advent of stereo, yet on close scrutiny they nearly always appeal to us with a deep humanity. Like certain other American-based conductors who suffered simply because they were not Arturo Toscanini, Mitropoulos' finest surviving performances are mostly those recorded with European orchestras (all unofficially). This is not to overlook fine Vaughan Williams, Schoenberg, Prokofiev and Shostakovich with the New York orchestra or the earlier 78s made in Minneapolis. The latter have so far been resurrected by the small but enterprising Nickson label, and clearly illustrate the pioneering work which Mitropoulos must have carried out, making the task of his successor in Minneapolis, Antal Dorati, that much easier. To represent Mitropoulos on the proverbial desert island I might turn to the Verdi operas "Ernani" or "La forza del destino" and to Puccini's "Tosca", but pride of place will probably go to the pioneering 1951 edition of Berg's "Wozzeck" which is shortly due for re-issue by Sony.

We come full circle with the apparently self-effacing Dutchman whose lot it was to take up Mengelberg's conducting responsibilities in Amsterdam. A few wartime 78s exist, but the main body of **Eduard van Beinum**'s work was an immediate postwar period with British Decca - he is heard on some of that company's very first LPs - followed by sessions with his native Philips company before meeting, like Abendroth and Mitropoulos, a comparatively early death. Van Beinum seems to have been a gentleman among conductors who eschewed personal intervention or point-making but who nevertheless brought out to its maximum the characteristic grain and homogeneity of the marvellous Concertgebouw Orchestra. His LP of the Berlioz "Symphonie fantastique", in its Ace of Clubs reissue, was one of the first and most frequent recordings on my modest turntable. Van Beinum's was an incomplete legacy, missing most of the Beethoven symphonies but calling out nonetheless for reassessment in our age of uniformity and mistrust of genuine individuality. To the Berlioz recording which I mentioned one might add, as representative of van Beinum at his best, works by Debussy, Ravel and Sibelius, various Bruckner symphonies and a tastefully proportioned Mahler Lied von der Erde.

Help with these discographies has come from many sources, as credited at the end of the book, but I must single out Stathis Arfanis, who despite having published his own Mitropoulos discography some years ago has been supportive and helpful in my project, to the extent of supplying copies of many of the record sleeves and concert programmes. A similar service has been performed by Roderick Krüsemann in the case of Mengelberg and van Beinum. I have also been greatly encouraged by Bill Flowers, who has contributed one of his inimitable postscripts for the Abendroth section. My grateful thanks to all of them.

The 3-column layout continues to be used for these discographies, which are arranged alphabetically by composer. Information in the first column indicates the city where the recording took place, followed now by a precise date wherever possible (day, month and year). Where a recording was spread over a period of time, only the first and last dates are given, but this does not always imply that sessions took place on all intervening days. Second column lists other artists taking part, such as singers, instrumentalists and orchestras (the only abbreviations needed for this volume were COA for (Royal) Amsterdam Concertgebouw Orchestra, NYPSO for both New York Philharmonic Symphony and New York Philharmonic, BPO for Berlin Philharmonic and LPO and LSO for London Philharmonic and London Symphony Orchestras respectively). The third column attempts to list as many catalogue numbers as possible for the main territories and for the principal formats of 78, EP (45), LP and CD (cassette tapes are not normally included). Information may not be complete for all overseas countries and I am always glad to hear from collectors who can add numbers or point out possible errors. Catalogue numbers which appear on the same line of text, usually separated by "/", often indicate the simultaneous mono and stereo editions of an LP which became customary in the 1950s and 1960s. For example, HMV had ALP (mono) and ASD (stereo), Columbia 33CX (mono) and SAX (stereo), Decca LXT (mono) and SXL (stereo), Victor/RCA LM and RB (mono) and LSC and SB (stereo), US Columbia ML (mono) and MS (stereo) and so on. It should also be borne in mind that some catalogue numbers may be for sets in which the work in question is grouped together with other pieces.

Willem Mengelberg
1871-1951

with valuable assistance from Roderick Krüsemann

Discography compiled by John Hunt

HENDRIK ANDRIESSEN (1892-1981)

Magna re est amor, for soprano and orchestra

Amsterdam 9 April 1940	COA Vincent	78: Telefunken SK 3085 LP: Past Masters PM 9 CD: Teldec ZS 844.157/243.7232

JOHANN CHRISTIAN BACH (1735-1782)

Sinfonia in B flat

Amsterdam 10 June 1927	COA	78: Columbia L 2047 78: Columbia (Italy) GQX 10488 78: Columbia (USA) 67473D 78: Columbia (Japan) J 7260 78: Decca (USA) 25014 78: Odeon 0-8338 78: Odeon (France) 123 531 78: Odeon (Australia) 0-4111 CD: Pearl GEMMCDS 9018 This recording comprises first and second movements only
New York 16 January 1929	NYPSO	78: Victor 7483-7484 78: HMV D 1988-1989/DB 10115-10116 78: Victor (Japan) JD 2017-2018/ ND 946-947 45: Victor CAE 387 LP: Victor RED 2021/CAL 336/CAL 347 CD: Pearl GEMMCD 9474

Piano Concerto in B flat

Amsterdam 21 March 1943	COA M.Flipse	CD: Archive Documents ADCD 112

JOHANN SEBASTIAN BACH (1685-1750)

Matthäus-Passion

Amsterdam 2 April 1939	COA Toonkunst Choir Vincent, Durigo, Tulder, Erb, Ravelli, Schey	LP: Philips A00320-00322L/ 6747 168 A00150-00153L/ABL 3035-3038 LP: Philips (Japan) FL 5561-5563 LP: Columbia (USA) SL 179 CD: Philips 416 2062/PHCP 1309-1311 Excerpts 45: Philips A400176E/A400177E/I113518E LP: Philips W09913L/G05301R/G05388R LP: Philips (Japan) PC 5557-5558 LP: Turnabout TV 4445-4446

Matthäus-Passion, excerpts (O Mensch bewein dein' Sünde; Erbarm' es Gott; O Haupt voll Blut und Wunden; Wenn ich einmal soll scheiden; Nun ist der Herr zur Ruh' gebracht; Wir setzen uns mit Tränen nieder)

Amsterdam 5 April 1936	COA Toonkunst Choir Vincent, Durigo, Erb, Ravelli	CD: Archive Documents ADCD 109

Cantata No 57 "Selig ist der Mann"

Amsterdam 7 November 1940	COA Toonkunst Choir Vincent, Kloos	LP: Archive Documents AD 103-104 CD: Seven Seas (Japan) KICC 2063

Cantata No 202 "Weichet nur betrübte Schatten"

Amsterdam 17 April 1939	COA Sluys	LP: Discocorp RR 234 CD: Seven Seas (Japan) KICC 2056

Piano Concerto in F minor

Amsterdam 17 April 1939	COA Jambor	CD: Archive Documents ADCD 112

Double Violin Concerto in D minor

Amsterdam 24 June 1935	COA Zimmerman, Hellmann	78: Decca K 20043-20044 LP: Discocorp RR 501 CD: Pearl GEMMCD 9154 CD: Biddulph WHL 024

Orchestral Suite No 2

Amsterdam 2 June 1931	COA	78: Columbia LX 134-136 78: Columbia (France) LFX 243-245 78: Columbia (Germany) LWX 328-330/ DWX 1576-1578 78: Columbia (Italy) GQX 10389-10391 78: Columbia (Holland) LHX 8045-8047 78: Columbia (USA) M 168/MM 168 78: Columbia (Japan) J 7891-7893/ JW 318-320/W 170-172 LP: Columbia (Japan) KT 1/3 LP: Discocorp RR 443 CD: Pearl GEMMCDS 9018
Amsterdam 17 April 1939	COA	LP: Discocorp RR 234 CD: Archive Documents ADCD 112 CD: Seven Seas (Japan) KICC 2056

Orchestral Suite No 3

Amsterdam Date not confirmed	COA	Unpublished radio broadcast

Air (Orchestral Suite No 3)

New York 16 January 1929	NYPSO	78: Victor 7484 78: HMV D 1989/DB 10116 45: Victor CAE 387 LP: Private issue (USA) P 1001 CD: Pearl GEMMCD 9474
Amsterdam 21 December 1937	COA	78: Telefunken SK 2402 78: Telefunken (Japan) 23661 78: Capitol 87006/EBL 8057 45: Capitol KBM 8057 LP: Past Masters PM 22 CD: Biddulph WHL 024

HENK BADINGS (1907-1987)

Symphony No 3

Amsterdam 2 May 1935	COA	Unpublished newsreel film Fragment only

BELA BARTOK (1881-1845)

Violin Concerto No 2

Amsterdam 23 March 1939	COA Szekely	LP: Hungaroton LPX 11573 CD: Philips 426 1042 World premiere performance

LUDWIG VAN BEETHOVEN (1770-1827)

Symphony No 1

New York 9 January 1930	NYPSO	78: Victor M 73/AM 73 78: HMV D 1867-1870/DB 4210-4213/ D 7268-7271 auto/D 7649-7652 auto 78: Electrola EJ 594-597 LP: Discocorp RR 501 LP: Archive Documents AD 105-106 CD: Biddulph WHL 020
Amsterdam 8 November 1938	COA	78: Telefunken SK 2770-2772 78: Ultraphon G 14701-14703 78: Supraphon G 22021-22023 78: Capitol ECL 8081 45: Capitol KCM 8081 LP: Telefunken LSK 7013/TYX 3-2 LP: Capitol P 8079 LP: Telefunken (Japan) MZ 5102 LP: Seven Seas (Japan) MH 5241/K17C 9508
Amsterdam 18 April 1940	COA	LP: Philips W09900L/6597 009/6767 003 LP: Philips (Japan) FL 5564 LP: Pearl HE 301 CD: Philips 416 2002
Amsterdam 18 March 1943	COA	Unpublished radio broadcast

KONZERTDIREKTION ARTHUR LASER, BERLIN-W1.

Berliner Musikfest 1913

:: **Beethoven-Feier** ::

Philharmonie: 9. — 10. — 12. — 16. Juni, abends 8 Uhr:

Fest-Dirigent:

Willem Mengelberg

Solisten:

Bronislaw **Hubermann**, Heinrich **Knote**,

Artur **Schnabel**,

Elisabeth **Ohlhoff**, Paula **Weinbaum**,

Felix **Senius**, Arthur van **Eweyk**

Philharmonisches Orchester :::: Bruno Kittel'scher Chor.

Prospekte und Karten zu 10, 8, 7, 6, 5, 4 und 2 Mark für jedes Konzert bei Bote & Bock und A. Wertheim.

THE

PHILHARMONIC

SOCIETY OF NEW YORK

··· FOUNDED 1842 ···

CARNEGIE HALL

SAT. EVE.
APR. 11
AT 8.00

METROPOLITAN OPERA HOUSE

TUES. EVE.
APR. 14
AT 8.00

WILLEM MENGELBERG

CONDUCTOR

TWO SPECIAL CONCERTS

BACH
ST. MATTHEW PASSION

FULL PHILHARMONIC ORCHESTRA
SCHOLA CANTORUM OF 250 VOICES
FATHER FINN'S PAULIST BOYS' CHOIR

ASSISTED BY

ELISABETH RETHBERG - SOPHIE BRASLAU - LAMBERT MURPHY
THOMAS DENYS - JOHN BARCLAY - WANDA LANDOWSKA

TICKETS FOR SATURDAY EVENING $1.50 TO $3.50 - TICKETS FOR TUESDAY EVENING $1.00 TO $3.50
AT RESPECTIVE BOX OFFICES

ARTHUR JUDSON
MANAGER

D. EDWARD PORTER
ASSOCIATE MANAGER

THE STEINWAY IS THE OFFICIAL PIANO OF THE PHILHARMONIC SOCIETY

Symphony No 2

Amsterdam 14 May 1936	COA	Unpublished radio broadcast
Amsterdam 21 April 1940	COA	LP: Philips W009901L/6597 009/6767 003 LP: Philips (Japan) FL 5565 CD: Philips 416 2002
Amsterdam 21 March 1943	COA	Unpublished radio broadcast

Symphony No 3 "Eroica"

New York 4-9 January 1930	NYPSO	78: Victor M 115/AM 115 78: HMV DB 1599-1608/DB 7502-7508 auto/ DB 7105-7111 auto LP: Victor LM 115/LAM 115/RED 2001 CD: Biddulph WHL 020
Amsterdam March 1938	COA	Unpublished radio broadcast
Amsterdam 11 November 1940	COA	78: Telefunken SK 3117-3122 78: Capitol 81706-81711/EFL 2502 45: Capitol 80006-80011/KFM 8002 LP: Telefunken LSK 7006/TYX 3-1 LP: Telefunken (Japan) MZ 5100 LP: Capitol P 8002 LP: Columbia (Japan) DXM 139 LP: Rococo 2003 LP: Seven Seas (Japan) MH 5241 LP: Philips 6597 011/6767 003 CD: Philips 416 2012
Amsterdam 14 April 1940	COA	Unpublished radio broadcast
Amsterdam 6 May 1943	COA	LP: Discocorp RR 234 CD: Music and Arts CD 780 CD: Seven Seas (Japan) KICC 2054 Music and Arts dated May 1943

Symphony No 4

Amsterdam 1-2 December 1938	COA	78: Telefunken SK 2794-2797 78: Ultraphon G 14708-14711 78: Supraphon G 22034-22037 78: Telefunken (Japan) 43608-43611 LP: Rococo 2011 LP: Ultraphon ULX 3009 LP: Telefunken (Japan) SLC 2327 CD: World Classics WC 44012
Amsterdam 25 April 1940	COA	LP: Philips W09902L/GL 5806/ 6597 012/6767 003 LP: Philips (Japan) FL 5566/SFON 10603 CD: Philips 416 2022

Symphony No 5

Amsterdam 4 April 1937	COA	78: Telefunken SK 2210-2213 78: Ultraphon G 14712-14715 78: Supraphon G 22038-22041 78: Capitol 87092-87095/EDL 8110 45: Capitol KDM 8110 LP: Capitol P 8110 LP: Telefunken LSK 7005/LK 7005 LP: Telefunken (Japan) MZ 5101 LP: Seven Seas (Japan) MH 5244 CD: Teldec 4509 955152/ZS 844.159/ 243.7252 4509 955152 incorrectly dated May 1937
Amsterdam 18 April 1940	COA	LP: Philips W09906L/G03111L/GL 5689/ 6597 016/6701 031/6767 003 LP: Philips (Japan) FL 5570/SFON 10599 CD: Philips 416 2022

Symphony No 5, First movement

Camden NJ 11-14 April 1922	NYPSO	78: Victor 1069 LP: Past Masters PM 6 CD: Biddulph WHL 025-026

Symphony No 6 "Pastoral"

Amsterdam 17 May 1936	COA	Unpublished radio broadcast
Amsterdam December 1937- January 1938	COA	78: Telefunken SK 2424-2428 78: Telefunken (France) T 49-53 78: Ultraphon G 14716-14720 LP: Telefunken (Japan) SLC 2326 LP: Musical Appreciation Society S 117 CD: Teldec ZS 844.162/243.7282
Amsterdam May 1938	COA	Unpublished radio broadcast
Amsterdam 14 April 1940	COA	LP: Philips W09903L/C73 AX204/ 6597 013/6767 003 LP: Philips (Japan) FL 5567/SFON 10597 CD: Philips 416 2032

Symphony No 7

Berlin 1939	Berlin RO	LP: Japan GMV 4 CD: Archive Documents ADCD 111
Amsterdam 25 April 1940	COA	LP: Philips W09904L/6597 014/6767 003 LP: Philips (Japan) FL 5568/SFON 10602 CD: Philips 416 2052

Symphony No 8

Amsterdam 9 November 1938	COA	78: Telefunken SK 2760-2762 78: Supraphon G 22052-22054 78: Ultraphon G 14721-14723 78: Ultraphon (Japan) 43601-43603 78: Polydor (France) 566258-566260 78: Capitol 87042-87044/ECL 8080 45: Capitol KCM 8080 LP: Capitol P 8079 LP: Telefunken LSK 7013/TYX 3-2 LP: Telefunken (Japan) MZ 5101 LP: Seven Seas (Japan) MH 5244 CD: Teldec 4509 955152/ZS 844.159/ 243.7252
Amsterdam 18 April 1940	COA	LP: Philips W09900L/6597 009/6767 003 LP: Philips (Japan) FL 5564/SFON 10603 CD: Philips 416 2042
Amsterdam 13 May 1943	COA	Unpublished radio broadcast

Symphony No 8, Second movement

Amsterdam 10 June 1927	COA	78: Columbia L 1973 78: Columbia (Italy) GQX 10461 78: Columbia (USA) 67421 78: Columbia (Japan) J 7197 78: Columbia (Australia) 4055 78: Odeon 0-8327/0-8398 78: Odeon (France) 123570 78: Decca (USA) 25235 LP: EMI 5C 047 01297M CD: Pearl GEMMCDS 9018

Concertgebouw
Donderdag 4 November 1937 te 8.15

Abonnementsconcert

serie A en B
dirigent: Willem Mengelberg

Luigi Cherubini
1760—1842

Ouverture „Anacreon"

Johannes Brahms
1833—1897

Concert (D gr. t., op. 77)
voor viool en orkest
Allegro non troppo
Adagio
Allegro giocoso
solist: Adolf Busch

Pauze

Gustav Mahler
1860—1911

Eerste symphonie (D gr. t.)
Langsam, schleppend — Frisch und belebt
Kräftig bewegt — Recht gemächlich (Trio)
Feierlich und gemessen — Sehr einfach und schlicht wie eine Volksweise
Finale

Concertgebouw
Donderdag 31 Maart 1938 te 8.15

Abonnementsconcert

serie A en B
dirigent: Willem Mengelberg

L. van Beethoven
1770—1827

Ouverture „Coriolan"

Johannes Brahms
1833—1897

Eerste concert d kl. t. (op. 15)
voor piano en orkest

Maestoso
Adagio
Rondo: Allegro non troppo

solist: Wilhelm Backhaus

Pauze

P. I. Tschaikowsky
1840—1893

Vijfde symphonie e kl. t. (op. 64)

Andante — Allegro con anima
Andante cantabile, con alcuna licenza
Valse: Allegro moderato
Finale: Andante maestoso — Allegro vivace

Symphony No 9 "Choral"

Amsterdam 31 May 1938	COA Toonkunst Choir Sluys, Luger, Tulder, Ravelli	CD: Archive Documents ADCD 113 CD: Music and Arts CD 918
Amsterdam 2 May 1940	COA Toonkunst Choir Sluys, Luger, Tulder, Ravelli	LP: Philips W09905-09906L/6597 015/ 6701 031/6767 003 LP: Philips (Japan) FL 5569-5570/ SFON 10593 CD: Philips 416 2052
Amsterdam 15 May 1942	COA Toonkunst Choir Bijster, Luger, Vroons, Ravelli	Unpublished radio broadcast
Amsterdam 13 May 1943	COA Toonkunst Choir Bijster, Luger, Tulder, Ravelli	Unpublished radio broadcast

Piano Concerto No 5 "Emperor"

Amsterdam 9 May 1942	COA De Groot	LP: Archive Documents AD 105-106 Recording incomplete

Violin Concerto

Amsterdam 18 April 1940	COA Zimmerman	Unpublished radio broadcast
Amsterdam May 1943	COA Bustabo	CD: Archive Documents ADCD 117 CD: Seven Seas (Japan) KICC 2060

Coriolan, overture

Camden NJ 11 April 1922	NYPSO	78: Victor 74756-74757/6223 78: HMV DB 369 LP: Past Masters PM 6 CD: Biddulph WHL 025-026
Amsterdam May 1926	COA	78: Columbia L 1848 78: Columbia (Italy) GQX 10371 78: Columbia (USA) 67273D 78: Columbia (Japan) J 7070 78: Odeon 0-8595 78: Odeon (France) 123863 78: Decca (USA) 25275 CD: Pearl GEMMCDS 9070
Amsterdam 1 June 1931	COA	78: Columbia LX 167 78: Columbia (France) LFX 261 78: Columbia (Japan) J 8042 78: Columbia (USA) 68049D 78: Odeon 0-8595 LP: Past Masters PM 20 LP: Discocorp RR 443 CD: Pearl GEMMCDS 9018

Egmont, overture

Amsterdam May 1926	COA	78: Columbia L 1799 78: Columbia (Italy) GQX 10349 78: Columbia (USA) 67220D 78: Columbia (Japan) J 7069 78: Odeon 0-8300 78: Odeon (France) 171006-171007/123865 78: Decca (USA) 25284 CD: Symposium SYMCD 1078 CD: Pearl GEMMCDS 9070
New York 14 January 1930	NYPSO	78: Victor 7291 78: Victor (Japan) VD 8010/ND 109 78: HMV D 1908/DB 6003 78: HMV (France) AW 216 78: Electrola EJ 651 LP: Victor CAL 347 CD: Pearl GEMMCDS 9474 2 takes of Side 1 were known to be in circulation
Amsterdam 2 June 1931	COA	78: Columbia LX 161 78: Columbia (France) LFX 260 78: Columbia (Germany) LWX 327/DWX 1573 78: Columbia (USA) 68048D 78: Columbia (Japan) J 8027/JW 375 LP: Past Masters PM 20 CD: Pearl GEMMCDS 9018
Amsterdam 9 November 1940	COA	Unpublished newsreel film Fragments only
Amsterdam 29 April 1943	COA	LP: Discocorp RR 234 CD: Music and Arts CD 780 CD: Seven Seas (Japan) KICC 2054
Amsterdam 13 or 23 April 1944	COA	Unpublished radio broadcast

Fidelio, overture

Amsterdam 28 April 1940	COA	Unpublished radio broadcast
Amsterdam 13 October 1940	COA	LP: Philips W09901L/6597 010/ 6767 003/6866 044 LP: Philips (Japan) FL 5565/SFON 10602 CD: Philips 416 2032 Issues of this performance have been variously dated April 1940 and November 1940

Die Geschöpfe des Prometheus, excerpts (Overture, Allegretto and Finale)

Amsterdam November 1942	COA	78: Capitol 86011 LP: Capitol P 8078 LP: Past Masters PM 20

Leonore No 1, overture

Amsterdam 2 June 1931	COA	78: Columbia LX 160 78: Columbia (Japan) J 7965/JW 376 78: Columbia (Australia) LOX 155 78: Columbia (USA) 68055D LP: Past Masters PM 20 CD: Symposium SYMCD 1078 CD: Pearl GEMMCDS 9018

Leonore No 3, overture

Amsterdam 30 May 1930	COA	78: Columbia LX 129-130 78: Columbia (France) LFX 187-188 78: Columbia (Germany) LWX 323-324/ DWX 5006-5007 78: Columbia (USA) X 40/MX 40 78: Columbia (Japan) J 7857-7858 78: Columbia (Australia) LOX 127-128 78: Columbia (Argentina) 264810-264811 LP: Columbia (Japan) KT 1-3 LP: Past Masters PM 20 CD: Pearl GEMMCDS 9018

Die Ruinen von Athen, Turkish march

Amsterdam 31 May 1930	COA	78: Columbia LX 130 78: Columbia (France) LFX 188 78: Columbia (Germany) LWX 324/DWX 5007 78: Columbia (USA) 67988D/70454 78: Columbia (Japan) J 7858/J 8176 78: Columbia (Australia) LOX 128 78: Columbia (Argentina) 264811 LP: Past Masters PM 20 Cassette: In Sync C 4130 CD: Pearl GEMMCDS 9018
Amsterdam November 1942	COA	78: Telefunken SK 3713 LP: Capitol P 8078

HECTOR BERLIOZ (1803-1869)

La damnation de Faust, Marche hongroise

Amsterdam May 1926	COA	78: Columbia L 1810 78: Columbia (Italy) GQX 10352 78: Columbia (Japan) J 7036 78: Odeon 0-8303/0-8381 78: Odeon (France) 171004 78: Decca (USA) 25220 LP: EMI 5C 047 01297M CD: EMI CDH 769 9562 CD: Pearl GEMMCDS 9018
Paris 30 April- 2 May 1931	COA	Unpublished video recording Filmed against backdrop of Concertgebouw Hall
Amsterdam April 1942	COA	78: Telefunken SK 3243 78: Telefunken (France) T 177 LP: Capitol L 8127 LP: Telefunken LB 6009 CD: Biddulph WHL 034 CD: Pearl GEMMCD 9154
Amsterdam 12 March 1943	COA	LP: Discocorp RR 234 CD: Seven Seas (Japan) KICC 2055

La damnation de Faust, Menuet des feux follets

Amsterdam April 1942	COA	78: Telefgunken SK 3242 LP: Telefunken LB 6009 LP: Capitol L 8127 CD: Biddulph WHL 023 CD: Pearl GEMMCD 9154
Amsterdam 12 March 1943	COA	LP: Discocorp RR 234 CD: Seven Seas (Japan) KICC 2055

La damnation de Faust, Menuet des sylphes

Amsterdam May 1926	COA	78: Columbia L 1810 78: Columbia (Italy) GQX 10352 78: Columbia (Japan) J 7036 78: Odeon 0-8303 78: Odeon (France) 171005 78: Decca (USA) 25220 LP: EMI 5C 047 01297M CD: EMI CDH 769 9562 CD: Pearl GEMMCDS 9018
Amsterdam April 1942	COA	78: Telefunken SK 3242 LP: Telefunken LB 6009 LP: Capitol L 8127 CD: Biddulph WHL 023 CD: Pearl GEMMCD 9154
Amsterdam 12 March 1943	COA	LP: Discocorp RR 234 CD: Seven Seas (Japan) KICC 2055

Le carnaval romain, overture

Amsterdam 21 December 1937	COA	78: Telefunken SK 2489 78: Telefunken (France) T 103 78: Ultraphon F 14265 78: Supraphon G 22415 78: Capitol 81002 78: Eurochord TAI 718 45: Capitol 6F-80023 LP: Rococo 2011 CD: Symposium SYMCD 1078 CD: Biddulph WHL 023

Un bal (Symphonie fantastique)

London 16 January 1938	BBCSO	Unpublished radio broadcast

GEORGES BIZET (1838-1875)

L'Arlésienne, Adagietto

Amsterdam June 1929	COA	78: Columbia DX 6/LCX 3 78: Columbia (Holland) D 15841 78: Columbia (USA) 67794D 78: Columbia (Japan) J 8176 LP: Past Masters PM 4 CD: Pearl GEMMCDS 9070
Paris 30 April- 2 May 1931	COA	Unpublished video recording Filmed against backdrop of Concertgebouw Hall

ERNEST BLOCH (1880-1959)

Violin Concerto

Amsterdam 9 November 1939	COA Szigeti	CD: Music and Arts CD 270

ALEXANDER BORODIN (1833-1887)

In the Steppes of Central Asia

Amsterdam April 1941	COA	78: Telefunken SK 3198 78: Telefunken (France) T 119 78: Capitol 80153 LP: Past Masters PM 4 CD: Archive Documents ADCD 108 CD: Pearl GEMMCD 9154

Klassiker der Musik

L. VAN BEETHOVEN

P. J. TSCHAIKOWSKY

WILLEM MENGELBERG
Concertgebouw-Orchester,
Amsterdam

Symphonie Nr. 5 c-moll
(L. van Beethoven)

Best.-Nr. SK 2210-13

Preis des Gesamtwerkes
(4 Platten)
einschließlich Ganzleinenalbum
RM 18,—

Symphonie Nr. 6 h-moll
(Pathétique)
(P. J. Tschaikowsky)

Best.-Nr. SK 2214-18

Preis des Gesamtwerkes
(5 Platten)
einschließlich Ganzleinenalbum
RM 22,50

EUGEN JOCHUM
Berliner Philharmoniker

Symphonie Nr. 7 A-dur
(L. van Beethoven)

Best.-Nr. SK 2763-67

Preis des Gesamtwerkes
(5 Platten)
einschließlich Ganzleinenalbum
RM 22,50

TELEFUNKEN Platten

JOHANNES BRAHMS (1833-1897)

Symphony No 1

Amsterdam 13 October 1940	COA	LP: Philips W09907L LP: Philips (Japan) FL 5603/SFON 10600 CD: Philips 416 2102 CD: Dante LYS 075 416 2102 dated December 1940
Amsterdam 13 April 1943	COA	Unpublished radio broadcast

Symphony No 1, Third movement

Amsterdam 31 May 1930	COA	78: Columbia LX 59 78: Columbia (Germany) LWX 247 78: Columbia GQX 10300 78: Columbia (USA) 67894D 78: Columbia (Japan) J 7807 78: Columbia (Australia) LOX 66 LP: Private issue (USA) P 1003 CD: Pearl GEMMCDS 9018

Symphony No 2

Amsterdam 1939	COA	CD: Dante LYS 125
Amsterdam 9 April 1940	COA	78: Telefunken SK 3075-3079 78: Capitol 87002-87026/EEL 8070 45: Capitol KEM 8070 LP: Capitol P 8070 LP: Telefunken HT 12/GMA 66 LP: Telefunken (Japan) MZ 5103 LP: Telefunken (USA) TH 97005 LP: Seven Seas (Japan) MH 5239 CD: Teldec ZS 844.156/243.7222 CD: Dante LYS 125

Symphony No 3

Amsterdam 10 May 1932	COA	78: Columbia LX 220-223/LX 8008-8011 auto 78: Columbia (France) LFX 305-308 78: Columbia (Italy) GQX 10688-10691 78: Columbia (USA) M 181 78: Columbia (Japan) J 8154-8157 78: Odeon 0 8800-8803 LP: Rococo 2051 LP: Imprimatur IMP 2 LP: EMI 1C 053 01453M CD: Pearl GEMMCDS 9018 CD: Dante LYS 088 Pearl is dated 1931 and Dante is dated 1941
Amsterdam 27 February 1944	COA	CD: Archive Documents ADCD 107 CD: Music and Arts CD 780 CD: Dante LYS 125

Symphony No 4

Amsterdam 29 November 1938	COA	78: Telefunken SK 2773-2777 LP: Telefunken HT 21/TYX 3-1 LP: Telefunken (USA) TH 97010 LP: Telefunken (Japan) MZ 5104 LP: Musical Appreciation Society S 116 LP: Past Masters PM 5 LP: Seven Seas (Japan) MH 5239 CD: Teldec ZS 844.158/243.7242 CD: Dante LYS 076

Violin Concerto

Amsterdam 13 April 1943	COA Krebbers	LP: Discocorp RR 234 CD: Music and Arts CD 780 CD: Seven Seas (Japan) KICC 2055 CD: Dante LYS 088

Academic Festival Overture

Amsterdam 30 May 1930	COA	78: Columbia LX 58-59 78: Columbia (Germany) LWX 246-247 78: Columbia (Italy) GQX 10299-10300 78: Columbia (USA) 67893-67894D/X 42 78: Columbia (Japan) J 7806-7807 78: Columbia (Australia) LOX 65-66 LP: EMI 1C 053 01453M LP: Imprimatur IMP 2 CD: EMI CDH 769 9562 CD: Pearl GEMMCDS 9018 CD: Dante LYS 076

Tragic Overture

Amsterdam April 1942	COA	78: Telefunken SK 3327-3328 78: Capitol 80070-80071/EBL 8014 45: Capitol KBM 8014 LP: Capitol P 8078 LP: Rococo 2051 LP: Discocorp RR 443 CD: Teldec ZS 844.156/243.7222 CD: Dante LYS 075

Ein deutsches Requiem

Amsterdam 7 November 1940	COA Toonkunst Choir Vincent, Kloos	LP: Philips W09912-09913L/FCM 32-33 LP: Philips (Japan) FL 5604-5605/ PC 5557-5558 LP: Turnabout TV 4445-4446 CD: Philips 416 2132 CD: Dante LYS 099

MAX BRUCH (1838-1929)

Violin Concerto No 1

Amsterdam 27 October 1940	COA Bustabo	LP: Rococo 2029 LP: Discocorp RR 506/BWS 1005 CD: Music and Arts CD 780 CD: Archive Documents ADCD 117 CD: Seven Seas (Japan) KICC 2060

LUIGI CHERUBINI (1760-1842)

Anacreon, overture

Amsterdam 10 June 1927	COA	78: Columbia L 1972-1973 78: Columbia (Italy) GQX 10460-10461 78: Columbia (USA) 67420-67421D/X 35 78: Columbia (Japan) J 7196-7197 78: Columbia (Australia) 4054-4055 78: Odeon O 8326-8327 78: Odeon (France) 123519-123520 78: Decca (USA) 25234-25235 LP: EMI 5C 047 01298M CD: EMI CDH 769 9562 CD: Pearl GEMMCDS 9018
Amsterdam 15 April 1943	COA	CD: Archive Documents ADCD 111 Incorrectly labelled as Berlin RO

FREDERIC CHOPIN (1810-1849)

Piano Concerto No 2

Amsterdam 9 April 1943	COA Van der Pas	CD: Archive Documents ADCD 114 CD: Theo van der Pas Stichting TPS 6901-6903 Opening section of first movement is missing from the recording

CLAUDE DEBUSSY (1862-1918)

Prélude à l'après-midi d'un faune

Amsterdam 30 November 1938	COA	78: Telefunken SK 2955 78: Ultraphon G 14208 78: Supraphon G 22172 LP: Past Masters PM 22 CD: Archive Documents ADCD 107 CD: Biddulph WHL 023

Fantaisie pour piano et orchestre

Amsterdam 6 October 1938	COA Gieseking	CD: Music and Arts CD 270/CD 780

CORNELIS DOPPER (1870-1939)

Symphony No 7 "Zuiderzeesymfonie"

Amsterdam 8 December 1940	COA	LP: Past Masters PM 16

Ciacona gotica

Amsterdam 9 April 1940	COA	78: Telefunken SK 3155-3157 78: Capitol 80123-80125/ECL 8031 45: Capitol KCM 8031 LP: Capitol P 8037 LP: Telefunken LSK 7012/LT 7012 LP: Rococo 2004 LP: Past Masters PM 9 CD: Teldec ZS 844.157/243.7232
Amsterdam 25 March 1943	COA	Unpublished radio broadcast

ANTONIN DVORAK (1841-1904)

Symphony No 9 "From the New World"

Amsterdam April 1941	COA	78: Telefunken SK 3190-3194 78: Ultraphon G 14280-14284 78: Supraphon G 80041-80045 LP: Private issue (Japan) M 1009 LP: Past Masters PM 4 CD: Teldec ZS 844.169/243.7312

Cello Concerto

Paris 16 January 1944	Paris RO Gendron	LP: Private issue (Japan) M 1009 LP: Past Masters PM 33 CD: Seven Seas (Japan) KICC 2058 CD: Archive Documents ADCD 116

CESAR FRANCK (1822-1890)

Symphony in D minor

Amsterdam 3 October 1940	COA	LP: Philips W 09908L LP: Philips (Japan) FL 5602 CD: Philips 416 2142 CD: Archive Documents ADCD 114
Amsterdam 12 November 1940	COA	78: Telefunken SK 3145-3149 78: Telefunken (France) T 142-146 78: Ultraphon G 80131-80135 78: Capitol 80089-80093/EEL 8023 45: Capitol KEM 8023 LP: Capitol P 8023 LP: Telefunken LSK 7001/LT 7001/ TYX 3-2 LP: Telefunken (Japan) MZ 5105 LP: Top Classic TC 007 LP: Seven Seas (Japan) MH 5245 CD: Biddulph WHL 023

Variations symphoniques pour piano et orchestre

Amsterdam 31 October 1940	COA Gieseking	LP: MRF Records MRF 74 LP: Discocorp IGI 358/MLG 70 CD: Seven Seas (Japan) KICC 2061 CD: Archive Documents ADCD 114

Psyché et Eros

Amsterdam December 1937- January 1938	COA	78: Telefunken SK 2463 78: Telefunken (Japan) J 73605/G 9068 78: Ultraphon G 14279 78: Supraphon G 22396 LP: Rococo 2011 CD: Archive Docments ADCD 107 CD: Biddulph WHL 023

CHRISTOPH WILLIBALD GLUCK (1714-1787)

Alceste, overture arranged by Mottl

Amsterdam 24 June 1935	COA	78: Decca K 771 78: Decca (USA) 25571 78: Grammophon 35024 78: Polydor (France) 516688 78: Polydor (Japan) 45236 78: Odeon (Argentina) 263500 LP: Rococo 2018 LP: Past Masters PM 22 CD: Symposium SYMCD 1078 CD: Koch 370112 It is possible that an alternative unpublished take also exists

EDVARD GRIEG (1843-1907)

2 Elegaic Melodies

Amsterdam 3 June 1931	COA	78: Columbia LX 168 78: Columbia (Germany) LWX 16 78: Columbia (USA) 68024D 78: Columbia (Japan) J 8002 LP: Columbia (Holland) 33HS 1003 LP: EMI 5C 047 01297M CD: EMI CDH 769 9562 CD: Pearl GEMMCDS 9070

Peer Gynt, suite No 1

Amsterdam 19 April 1943	COA	LP: Rococo 2066 CD: Archive Documents ADCD 108

JOHAN HALVORSEN (1864-1935)

March of the Boyars

Camden NJ 16 April 1924	NYPSO	78: Victor 74905/6464 78: HMV DB 804 LP: Past Masters PM 7 CD: Biddulph WHL 025-026

GEORGE FRIDERIC HANDEL (1685-1759)

Alcina, suite arranged by Göhler

New York 16 January 1929	NYPSO	78: Victor 1435-1436 78: Victor (Japan) JE 187-188/ NF 4065-4066/JAS 99 78: HMV E 548-549 78: Electrola EW 84-85 LP: Archive Documents AD 105-106 CD: Pearl GEMMCD 9474

Messiah, Allelujah Chorus

Amsterdam 7 May 1938	COA Toonkunst Choir	LP: Archive Documents AD 103-104 CD: Seven Seas (Japan) KICC 2056

PAUL HINDEMITH (1895-1963)

Violin Concerto

Amsterdam 14 March 1940	COA Helmann	CD: Archive Documents ADCD 110 World premiere performance

ENGELBERT HUMPERDINCK (1854-1921)

Hänsel und Gretel, overture

New York 14 January 1930	NYPSO	78: Victor 7436 78: HMV D 1950 78: HMV (France) AW 242 LP: Victor CAL 347/RED 2021 CD: Pearl GEMMCD 9474

ZOLTAN KODALY (1882-1967)

Hary Janos, suite

Amsterdam 12 December 1940	COA	LP: MRF Records MRF 74 LP: Rococo 2059 CD: Seven Seas (Japan) KICC 2062 CD: Archive Documents ADCD 115

Peacock Variations

Amsterdam 23 November 1939	COA	LP: MRF Records MRF 74 LP: Rococo 2059 LP: Past Masters PM 37 CD: Seven Seas (Japan) KICC 2062 CD: Archive Documents ADCD 115 Archive Documents dated December 1940

Concertgebouw

Donderdag 23 November 1939 te 8.15

Abonnementsconcert

serie A en B

dirigent: Willem Mengelberg

Robert Schumann
1810—1856

Ouverture „Manfred"

Gustav Mahler
1860—1911

Lieder eines fahrenden Gesellen
voor zang en orkest

solist: Hermann Schey

Zoltán Kodály
geb. 1882

** Fölszállott a páva
Variaties over een Hongaarsch volkslied

Pauze

Max Reger
1873—1916

* Hymnus der Liebe, op. 136
voor bariton en orkest

solist: Hermann Schey

Richard Wagner
1813—1883

Voorspel en slotscène uit „Tristan und Isolde"

** *allereerste uitvoering*

* *eerste uitvoering*

6-21 MEI 1920

TER GELEGENHEID VAN HET 25 JARIG JUBILEUM

VAN

WILLEM MENGELBERG

ALS

DIRIGENT VAN HET CONCERTGEBOUW

F.B.

FRANZ LISZT (1811-1886)

Piano Concerto No 1

Amsterdam 27 February 1944	COA M.Flipse	CD: Archive Documents ADCD 114

Hungarian Fantasia for piano and orchestra

Breslau 1942-1943	Breslau RO Backhaus	LP: Japan GMV 4 LP: Archive Documents AD 105-106

Les Préludes

Camden NJ 18-20 April 1922	NYPSO	78: Victor 74780-74782 and 66131/ 6225 and 6373 78: HMV DB 371 and 852 LP: Past Masters PM 6 CD: Biddulph WHL 025-026
Amsterdam June 1929	COA	78: Columbia L 2362-2363 78: Columbia (Germany) LWX 244-245/ W 181-182 78: Columbia (Japan) J 7611-7612 78: Columbia (USA) X 29/MX 29 78: Columbia (Argentina) 264817-264818 78: Odeon O 8402-8403 78: Odeon (France) 123861-123862 78: Odeon (Australia) O 4380-4381 78: Decca (USA) 25438-25439 LP: Rococo 2012 LP: EMI 5C 047 01297M CD: EMI CDH 769 9562 CD: Archive Documents ADCD 107 CD: Pearl GEMMCDS 9018

GUSTAV MAHLER (1860-1911)

Symphony No 4

Amsterdam 9 November 1939	COA Vincent	LP: Philips W09911L/A02847L/PHM 500040/ C73 AX204 LP: Philips (Japan) FL 5600/SFON 10598 LP: Turnabout TV 4425 LP: Melodiya M10 44436 006 CD: Philips 416 2112/426 1082

Adagietto (Symphony No 5)

Amsterdam May 1926	COA	78: Columbia L 1798 78: Columbia (Japan) J 7032 78: Odeon 0-8591 78: Decca (USA) 25011 LP: MRF Records MRF 74 LP: EMI 5C 047 01297M CD: EMI CDH 769 9562 CD: Pearl GEMMCDS 9070 CD: Symposium SYMCD 1078

Lieder eines fahrenden Gesellen

Amsterdam 23 November 1939	COA	LP: MRF Records MRF 74 LP: Private issue (Japan) M 5003/GMV 7 LP: Discocorp RR 506 LP: Private issue (Netherlands) 6818 754 LP: Archive Documents AD 103-104 CD: Archive Documents ADCD 116 CD: Seven Seas (Japan) KICC 2063 CD: Luister (Holland) CD 955

FELIX MENDELSSOHN-BARTHOLDY (1809-1847)

A Midsummer Night's Dream, overture

London 16 January 1938	BBCSO	CD: Archive Documents ADCD 111 CD: Dante LYS 089

A Midsummer Night's Dream, scherzo

Amsterdam 12 May 1928	COA	78: Columbia (Holland) D 41003 78: Columbia (France) DFX 97 78: Columbia (USA) 67486D/9560 78: Columbia (Japan) J 7323 78: Odeon O-8734 78: Decca (USA) 25523 LP: Columbia (Holland) 33HS 1003 CD: EMI CDH 769 9562 CD: Pearl GEMMCDS 9018/GEMMCDS 9070 2 different takes of this performance in circulation: the Pearl editions contain both, one in each set
London 16 January 1938	BBCSO	CD: Archive Documents ADCD 111 CD: Dante LYS 089

A Midsummer Night's Dream, nocturne

London 16 January 1938	BBCSO	CD: Archive Documents ADCD 111 CD: Dante LYS 089

War March of the Priests (Athalie)

Camden NJ 16 April 1924	NYPSO	78: Victor 74904/6464 78: HMV DB 804 LP: Past Masters PM 7 CD: Biddulph WHL 025-026 CD: Dante LYS 089 Arrangement by Halvone
New York 16 January 1929	NYPSO	78: Victor 7104 78: Victor (Japan) JD 1659 78: HMV D 1716 78: Electrola EJ 570 CD: Pearl GEMMCD 9474 Arrangement by Meyerbeer

RUDOLF MENGELBERG (1892-1959)

Praeludium on the Dutch National Anthem

Camden NJ 14 April 1924	NYPSO	CD: Biddulph WHL 025-026 CD: Pearl GEMMCDS 9922
Amsterdam 20 December 1936	COA	Unpublished radio broadcast
Amsterdam 30 November 1938	COA	78: Telefunken A 2899 78: Telefunken (Holland) NK 1965 45: Telefunken (Holland) U 55220 LP: MRF Records MRF 74 LP: Past Masters PM 9 CD: Teldec ZS 844.157/243.7232

Salve regina, arranged by Andriessen

Amsterdam 9 April 1940	COA Vincent	78: Telefunken SK 3084-3085 LP: Past Masters PM 9 CD: Teldec ZS 844.157/243.7232

GIACOMO MEYERBEER (1791-1864)

Coronation March (Le prophète), arranged by Mendelssohn

New York 15 January 1929	NYPSO	78: Victor 7104 78: Victor (Japan) JD 1659 78: HMV D 1716 78: Electrola EJ 570 CD: Biddulph WHL 024 CD: Pearl GEMMCD 9474

WOLFGANG AMADEUS MOZART (1756-1791)

Piano Concerto No 19

Amsterdam 13 October 1940	COA Andriessen	LP: Discocorp RR 234 CD: Seven Seas (Japan) KICC 2057

Flute Concerto No 2

Amsterdam 3 May 1942	COA Barwahser	LP: Discocorp RR 234 CD: Seven Seas (Japan) KICC 2057

Eine kleine Nachtmusik

Amsterdam November 1942	COA	78: Telefunken SK 3750-3751/ E 3750-3751 LP: Discocorp RR 501 CD: Archive Documents ADCD 112 CD: Pearl GEMMCD 9154

Exsultate jubilate

Amsterdam 5 March 1942	COA Ginster	LP: Discocorp RR 234 CD: Archive Documents ADCD 109 CD: Seven Seas (Japan) KICC 2057

Bella mia fiamma, concert aria

Amsterdam 5 March 1942	COA Ginster	Unpublished radio broadcast This recording is listed on Archive Documents CD ADCD 109 but is not contained on the disc

Die Zauberflöte, overture

New York 14 January 1930	NYPSO	78: Victor 1486 78: Victor (Japan) NF 4059 78: HMV E 564 LP: Victor CAL 347/RED 2021 CD: Pearl GEMMCD 9474
Amsterdam 3 May 1942	COA	LP: Private issue (Japan) GMV 5 LP: Archive Documents AD 103-104 CD: Archive Documents ADCD 116

HANS PFITZNER (1869-1949)

Cello Concerto

Amsterdam 12 December 1940	COA Cassado	LP: Rococo 2058 LP: Past Masters PM 33 CD: Seven Seas (Japan) KICC 2062

GIACOMO PUCCINI (1858-1924)

Madama Butterfly, excerpt (Un bel dì)

Amsterdam 23 June 1936	COA G.Moore	LP: Private issue (Japan) GMV 51 CD: Archive Documents ADCD 109

SERGEI RACHMANINOV (1873-1943)

Piano Concerto No 2

Amsterdam 31 October 1940	COA Gieseking	LP: MRF Records MRF 74 LP: Discocorp MJA 19693/IGI 353/RR 234 LP: Rococo 2029 LP: International Piano Library IPL 506 CD: Music and Arts CD 250

Piano Concerto No 3

Amsterdam 28 March 1940	COA Gieseking	LP: Discocorp IGI 358 LP: International Piano Library IPL 505 LP: Columbia (Japan) OZ 7563 CD: Music and Arts CD 250

Konzert-Bureau EMIL GUTMANN
Berlin W 35 Karlsbad 33

ZIRKUS SCHUMANN

Erste Aufführung:
Freitag, den 17. Mai 1912, abends 8 Uhr

Zweite Aufführung:
Sonnabend, den 18. Mai 1912, abends 8 Uhr

Gustav Mahler: VIII. Symphonie

in zwei Teilen
für Soli, Chöre, Orchester und Orgel

I. Teil: Hymnus „Veni creator spiritus"
II. Teil: Goethes Faust, II. Teil (Schlußszene)

Orgel beigestellt und eingebaut von E. F. Walker, Hoforgelbaumeister, Ludwigsburg, Wttbg.
Harmonium und Celesta beigestellt von Carl Simon, Harmoniumhaus, Berlin W 35.

Ein Teil des Reinertrages wird der Gustav Mahler-Stiftung zugeführt.

Konzert-Bureau EMIL GUTMANN, Berlin-München

Ausführende:

Musikalische Leitung:

Erste Aufführung: Freitag, 17. Mai, abends 8 Uhr.

WILLEM MENGELBERG

Dirigent des Concertgebouws Amsterdam und der Museumskonzerte Frankfurt a. M.

Zweite Aufführung: Sonnabend, 18. Mai, abends 8 Uhr.

DR. GEORG GÖHLER

Dirigent des Riedelvereins und der Musikalischen Gesellschaft Leipzig.

Soli:

Gertrude Förstel . . . . I. Sopran (auch Una poenitentium)
k. k. Hofopernsängerin, Wien

Martha Winternitz-Dorda . . . II. Sopran (auch Magna Peccatrix und Mater gloriosa)
Stadttheater, Hamburg

Ottilie Metzger . . . . . . I. Alt (auch Mulier Samaritana)
Stadttheater, Hamburg

Anna Erler Schnaudt . . . . II. Alt (auch Mater Aegyptiaca)
München

Felix Senius . . . . Tenor (auch Doctor Marianus)
Kammersänger, Berlin

Nicola Geisse-Winkel . . . . Bariton (auch Pater Ecstaticus)
Hofopernsänger, Wiesbaden

Wilhelm Fenten . . . . Baß (auch Pater profundus)
Hofopernsänger, Mannheim

Chöre:

I. Chor: Mitglieder der Chorvereinigungen, Leipzig: **Gewandhauschor, Universitäts-Kirchenchor St. Pauli.**

II. Chor: **Der Riedelverein Leipzig.**

III. Chor: **Hastung'scher Knabenchor**, Berlin.

Orchester:

Das verstärkte Berliner Philharmonische Orchester.

Orchesterbesetzung: 2 kleine und 4 große Flöten, 4 Oboen, Englischhorn, 2 Es-Klarinetten, 3 Klarinetten, Baßklarinette, 4 Fagotte, Kontrafagott, 8 Hörner, 4 Trompeten, 4 Posaunen, Baßtuba, 4 Harfen, Mandolinen, Celesta, Klavier, Harmonium, Pauken, große Trommel, Becken, Tamtam, Triangel, tiefe Glocken, Glockenspiel — Streichquintett. Isoliert postiert: 4 Trompeten, 3 Posaunen.

Orgel:

Max Fest, Leipzig.

MAURICE RAVEL (1875-1937)

Bolero

Amsterdam 31 May 1930	COA	78: Columbia LX 48-49 78: Columbia (Germany) LWX 310-311 78: Columbia (France) LFX 90-91 78: Columbia (Italy) GQX 10639-10640 78: Columbia (USA) X 22/MX 22 78: Columbia (Japan) J 7718-7719 78: Columbia (Canada) 15141-15142 78: Columbia (Australia) LOX 60-61 78: Columbia (Argentina) 264812-264813 LP: Discocorp RR 443 LP: Rococo 2012 CD: Pearl GEMMCDS 9070

Daphnis et Chloé, Second suite

Amsterdam 6 October 1938	COA	LP: MRF Records MRF 74 LP: Rococo 2066 LP: Discocorp RR 506 CD: Seven Seas (Japan) KICC 2061 CD: Archive Documents ADCD 115

The existence of unpublished radio broadcasts of La valse and Ma mère l'oye could not be confirmed

JULIUS ROENTGEN (1855-1932)

Old Dutch Dances

Amsterdam 10 November 1940	COA	45: Philips DE 99273 LP: MRF Records MRF 74 CD: Colofon (Holland) COLOFON-4
Amsterdam 19 April 1943	COA	Unpublished radio broadcast

CAMILLE SAINT-SAENS (1835-1921)

Le rouet d'Omphale, symphonic poem

Camden NJ 23 April 1923	NYPSO	78: Victor 66222-66223/989 78: HMV DA 665 CD: Biddulph WHL 025-026
New York 15 January 1929	NYPSO	78: Victor 7006 78: HMV D 1704 78: Electrola EJ 569 LP: Victor CAL 347/RED 2021 CD: Pearl GEMMCD 9474

ERNEST SCHELLING (1876-1939)

A Victory Ball, symphonic poem

New York 9 October 1925	NYPSO	78: Victor 1127-1128 LP: Archive Documents AD 105-106 CD: Biddulph WHL 025-026 CD: Pearl GEMMCDS 9922

FRANZ SCHUBERT (1797-1828)

Symphony No 8 "Unfinished"

Amsterdam 27 November 1939	COA	LP: Philips W09910L/G03111L/ GL 5698/6866 044 LP: Philips (Japan) FL 5585/SFON 10599 CD: Philips 416 2122
Amsterdam November 1942	COA	78: Telefunken SK 3352-3354/ E 3352-3354 LP: Past Masters PM 22 CD: Pearl GEMMCD 9154 CD: Dante LYS 077

Symphony No 9 "Great"

Amsterdam 19 December 1940	COA	LP: Philips W09909L/PHM 500041/ SPS4-905 LP: Philips (Japan) FL 5601 CD: Philips 416 2122 CD: Dante LYS 077
Amsterdam November 1942	COA	78: Telefunken SK 3341-3346 78: Capitol 80134-80140/EGL 8039 45: Capitol KGM 8039 LP: Capitol P 8040

Arpeggione Sonata, arranged by Cassado

Amsterdam 12 December 1940	COA Cassado	LP: Private issue (Japan) GMV 7 LP: Archive Documents AD 103-104 CD: Music and Arts CD 780 CD: Seven Seas (Japan) KICC 2063

Marche militaire, arrangement

Amsterdam April 1942	COA	78: Telefunken SK 3243/SK 3244 78: Telefunken (France) T 177 CD: Pearl GEMMCD 9154

Rosamunde, overture

Camden NJ 17 April 1924	NYPSO	78: Victor 6479 78: HMV DB 857 LP: Past Masters PM 7 CD: Biddulph WHL 025-026 Abridged version
Amsterdam 30 November 1938	COA	78: Telefunken SK 3008 78: Capitol 86006 LP: Capitol P 8078 LP: Rococo 2018 CD: Symposium SYMCD 1078
Amsterdam 27 November 1941	COA	LP: Philips W09910L LP: Philips (Japan) FL 5605 LP: Pearl HE 301 CD: Philips 416 2102

Rosamunde, Entr'acte No 3

Camden NJ 26 April 1923	NYPSO	78: Victor 6479 78: HMV DB 857 LP: Past Masters PM 6 CD: Biddulph WHL 025-026 Abridged version
Amsterdam 27 November 1941	COA	LP: Philips W09910L LP: Philips (Japan) FL 5605 LP: Pearl HE 301 CD: Philips 416 2102 CD: Archive Documents ADCD 114

Rosamunde, Ballet music no 1

Amsterdam 27 November 1941	COA	CD: Archive Documents ADCD 114

Rosamunde, Ballet music No 2

Amsterdam 27 November 1941	COA	LP: Philips W09910L LP: Philips (Japan) FL 5605 LP: Pearl HE 301 CD: Philips 416 2102 CD: Archive Documents ADCD 114

Rosamunde, Romanze (Der Vollmond strahlt)

Amsterdam 19 December 1940	COA Bosch-Schmidt	CD: Archive Documents ADCD 109

Claudine von Villabella, excerpt (Liebe schwärmt auf allen Wegen)

Amsterdam 19 December 1940	COA Bosch-Schmidt	CD: Archive Documents ADCD 109

Ständchen

Amsterdam 19 December 1940	COA Bosch-Schmidt	CD: Archive Documents ADCD 109

Vedi quanto adoro

Amsterdam 19 December 1940	COA Bosch-Schmidt	CD: Archive Documents ADCD 109

ROBERT SCHUMANN (1810-1856)

Piano Concerto

Amsterdam 10 October 1940	COA Sauer	LP: MRF Records MRF 74 LP: Private issue (Japan) M 1004 LP: Discocorp OP 78 LP: Melodiya M10 44947 004 CD: Seven Seas (Japan) KICC 2061

Richard Strauss
..Festival..

Under the Management of

Mr. HUGO GÖRLITZ

119, New Bond Street, London, W.

JUNE 3rd
TO
JUNE 9th
1903

Richard Strauss Festival

FOURTH CONCERT

Tuesday, June 9th, at 8 p.m.

"AUS ITALIEN" Op. 16 (Two Movements)
Neapolitanisches Volksleben
Am Strande von Sorrent

BURLESKE for Pianoforte and Orchestra

Herr WILHELM BACKHAUS

GUNTRAM

Prelude. Act I.
Friedenserzählung (The Vision of Peace)
for Tenor
Prelude. Act II.
Last Scene of Act III., for Tenor

Vocalist - Mr. JOHN HARRISON

"EIN HELDENLEBEN," Op. 40
Solo Violin - Herr ZIMMERMANN

Conductors:

RICHARD STRAUSS and WILLEM MENGELBERG

The Concertgebouw Symphonic Orchestra from Amsterdam

JOHANN STRAUSS II (1825-1899)

An der schönen blauen Donau, waltz abridged

New York January 1927	NYPSO	Brunswick unpublished

G'schichten aus dem Wienerwald, waltz abridged

Camden NJ 23 April 1923	NYPSO	78: Victor 74845/6427 78: HMV DB 805 LP: Past Masters PM 7 CD: Biddulph WHL 025-026
New York 10 January 1927	NYPSO	78: Brunswick 50096/20872 CD: Pearl GEMMCDS 9922

Künstlerleben, waltz abridged

New York 10 January 1927	NYPSO	78: Brunswick 50096/20872 CD: Pearl GEMMCDS 9922

Perpetuum mobile, arrangement

Amsterdam 11 May 1932	COA	78: Columbia LX 240 78: Columbia (Italy) GQX 10725 78: Columbia (Japan) J 8527 78: Columbia (USA) 9076M 78: Columbia (Australia) LOX 181 78: Columbia (Canada) 15182 LP: Rococo 2012 CD: Beulah 2PD 4 CD: Pearl GEMMCDS 9070

Wiener Blut, waltz abridged

New York January 1927	NYPSO	Brunswick unpublished

RICHARD STRAUSS (1864-1949)

Ein Heldenleben

New York 11-13 December 1928	NYPSO	78: Victor M 44/AM 44 78: HMV D 1711-1715/D 7321-7325 auto/ D 7653-7657 auto 78: HMV (Spain) AB 586-590 78: Electrola EJ 546-550 LP: Victor LM 44/LAM 44/CAL 337/ RED 2012/SMA 7001 CD: RCA/BMG 09026 609292
New York 11-13 December 1928	NYPSO	CD: Biddulph WHL 025-026 <u>Second performance comprising unissued takes</u>
Amsterdam April 1941	COA	78: Telefunken SK 3181-3185 78: Capitol 80054-80058/EEL 8013 45: Capitol KEM 8013 LP: Capitol P 8013 CD: Teldec ZS 844.163/243.7292/ 9031 764412

Don Juan

Amsterdam 8-9 November 1938	COA	78: Telefunken SK 2743-2744 78: Telefunken (France) T 140-141 78: Supraphon G 22481-22482/TF754-755 78: Mercury DM 24 LP: Mercury MG 15000 LP: Rococo 2018 LP: Telefunken (Japan) SLC 2326 CD: Teldec ZS 844.158/243.7242/ 9031 764412
Amsterdam 12 December 1940	COA	LP: Philips W09908L/FCM 20/6866 044 LP: Philips (Japan) FL 5602 LP: Rococo 2066 CD: Philips 416 2142

Tod und Verklärung

Amsterdam 14 April 1942	COA	78: Telefunken SK 3738-3740 LP: Capitol P 8100 LP: Telefunken LSK 7003/LE 6517/LGX 66032 LP: Telefunken (Japan) MZ 5102/K17C 9508 LP: Seven Seas (Japan) MH 5245

FRANZ VON SUPPE (1819-1895)

Poet and Peasant, overture

Amsterdam 11 May 1932	COA	78: Columbia LX 179 78: Columbia (Germany) LWX 21 78: Columbia (France) LFX 290 78: Columbia (Italy) GQX 10720 78: Columbia (USA) 50345/9075M 78: Columbia (Canada) 15132 78: Columbia (Japan) J 8096/W 19 78: Columbia (Australia) LOX 169 LP: Discocorp RR 443 LP: Columbia (Japan) KT 1-3 CD: Pearl GEMMCDS 9070

PIOTR TCHAIKOVSKY (1840-1893)

Symphony No 4

Amsterdam June 1929	COA	78: Columbia L 2336-2370 78: Columbia (Italy) GQX 10923-10927 78: Columbia (USA) M 133 78: Columbia (Japan) J 7615-7619 78: Columbia (Australia) LOX 6-10 78: Odeon O 8404-8408 78: Decca (USA) 25432-25436 LP: Rococo 2030 LP: Toshiba HA 5114/GR 2191/AB 9095 LP: Pearl GEMM 212-213 CD: Pearl GEMMCDS 9070 CD: Music and Arts CD 809 CD: Dante LYS 132

Symphony No 5

New York January 1926	NYPSO	Brunswick unpublished
Amsterdam 10 May 1928	COA	78: Columbia L 2176-2182 78: Columbia (Italy) GQX 10936-10942 78: Columbia (USA) M 104 78: Columbia (Japan) J 7313-7319/ JW 419-425/8045-8051 78: Columbia (Argentina) C-13 78: Odeon 0 8357-8363 78: Odeon (Australia) 0 4228-4234 78: Decca (USA) 25478-25484 LP: Discocorp RR 421 LP: Pearl GEMM 212-213 CD: Pearl GEMMCDS 9070 CD: Music and Arts CD 809
Amsterdam 26 November 1939	COA	LP: Discocorp RR 425 CD: Seven Seas (Japan) KICC 2059 CD: Music and Arts CD 780 CD: Dante LYS 137 Opening bars spliced in from 1928 Columbia recording; bars missing from second movement
Berlin 5-6 July 1940	BPO	78: Telefunken SK 3086-3091 78: Capitol EFL 8053 45: Capitol KFM 8053/EFM 8090 LP: Capitol P 8053 LP: Telefunken HT 4/GM 69/KT 11010/ DP 648.014 LP: Telefunken (USA) TH 97001 LP: Telefunken (Japan)MZ5106/TYX3-2 LP: Seven Seas (Japan) MH 5242 CD: Teldec ZS 844.161/243.7272 CD: Dante LYS 189

Symphony No 5, Second and third movements

Amsterdam 10 June 1927	COA	78: Odeon (France) 123533-123535 CD: Pearl GEMMCDS 9070

Concertgebouw
Donderdag 9 November 1939 te 8.15

Abonnementsconcert

serie A en B
dirigent: Willem Mengelberg

Chr. W. von Gluck 1714—1787 — Ouverture „Alceste"

Ernest Bloch geb. 1880 — * Concert
voor viool en orkest
Allegro deciso
Andante
Deciso

solist: Joseph Szigéti

Pauze

Gustav Mahler 1860—1911 — Vierde symphonie G gr. t.
Heiter, bedächtig
In gemächlicher Bewegung — Ohne Hast
Ruhevoll (Poco Adagio)
Sehr behaglich

sopraan-solo: Jo Vincent

* *eerste uitvoering*

Concertgebouw

Donderdag 28 Maart 1940 te 8.15

Abonnementsconcert

serie A en B

dirigent: Willem Mengelberg

Bedřich Smetana
1824—1884

Ouverture „Prodaná Nevěsta"

Sergei Rachmaninoff
geb. 1873

Derde concert d kl. t., op. 30
voor piano en orkest

Allegro ma non tanto
Intermezzo: Adagio
Finale: Alla breve

solist: Walter Gieseking

Pauze

P. I. Tschaikowsky
1840—1893

Zesde symphonie b kl. t., op. 74
„Pathétique"

Adagio — Allegro non troppo — Andante
Allegro con grazia
Allegro molto vivace
Finale: Adagio lamentoso

*Grotrian-Steinweg Concertvleugel
van C. C. Bender, Spui 12*

Symphony No 6 "Pathétique"

Amsterdam 3-4 April 1937	COA	Telefunken unpublished
Amsterdam 21 December 1937	COA	78: Telefunken SK 2214-2218 78: Telefunken (Japan) 23681-23685 78: Ultraphon G 14214-14218 78: Ultraphon (Japan) G 9000-9004 LP: Telefunken HT 3/GMA 52/KT 11010/ DP 648.014 LP: Telefunken (Japan) MZ 5107 LP: Telefunken (USA) TH 97002 LP: Musical Appreciation Society S 114 LP: Philharmonic (USA) 44 LP: Seven Seas (Japan) MH 5242 CD: Music and Arts CD 809 CD: Teldec ZS 844.164/243.7302 CD: Dante LYS 175
Amsterdam 22 April 1941	COA	78: Telefunken SK 3176-3180 78: Capitol 87087-87091 45: Capitol KEM 8103 LP: Capitol P 8103 CD: Archive Documents ADCD 108 CD: Teldec 4509 936732 This 1941 recording used the same 78rpm matrix numbers as the 1937 version

Symphony No 6 "Pathétique", Second movement abridged

Camden NJ 19 April 1923	NYPSO	78: Victor 74816/6374 78: HMV DB 465 LP: Past Masters PM 7 CD: Biddulph WHL 025-026

Symphony No 6 "Pathétique", Fourth movement abridged

Camden NJ 23 April 1923	NYPSO	78: Victor 74817/6374 78: HMV DB 465 LP: Past Masters PM 7 CD: Biddulph WHL 025-026

Piano Concerto No 1

Berlin 5-6 July 1940	BPO Hansen	78: Telefunken SK 3092-3095 78: Telefunken (France) T 76-79 78: Ultraphon G 14273-14276 LP: Capitol P 8097 LP: Past Masters PM 18 LP: Private issue (Japan) M 1003 CD: Teldec ZS 844.160/243.7262

Romeo and Juliet, Fantasy overture

Amsterdam 30 May 1930	COA	78: Columbia LX 55-56 78: Columbia (Germany) LWX 321-322/ DWX 5004-5005 78: Columbia (Japan) J 7877-7878 78: Columbia (USA) X 33/MX 33 78: Columbia (Australia) LOX 62-63 78: Columbia (Canada) 15147-15148/ 15699-15700 78: Columbia (Argentina) 266319-266320 LP: Columbia (USA) RL 3039 LP: Rococo 2018 LP: EMI 5C 047 01298M CD: Pearl GEMMCDS 9070 CD: Music and Arts CD 809 CD: Dante LYS 132

Marche slave

New York 4 January 1926	NYPSO	78: Brunswick 50072/A 73033/ B 20822-20823 78: Polydor (France) 595017 LP: Archive Documents AD 105-106 CD: Symposium SYMCD 1078 CD: Pearl GEMMCDS 9922

Serenade for strings

Amsterdam 9 October 1938	COA	LP: Discocorp RR 425 CD: Seven Seas (Japan) KICC 2059 CD: Dante LYS 137 Opening bars missing from the recording
Amsterdam 7 November 1938	COA	78: Telefunken SK 2901-2903 78: Ultraphon G 14219-14221 78: Supraphon G 22015-22017 LP: Capitol P 8060 LP: Rococo 2004 LP: Telefunken (Japan) SLC 2327 CD: Teldec ZS 844.160/243.7262 CD: Biddulph WHL 024 CD: Dante LYS 189

Waltz (Serenade for strings)

Camden NJ 26 April 1923	NYPSO	78: Victor 74844/6427 78: HMV DB 805 LP: Past Masters PM 7 CD: Biddulph WHL 025-026
Amsterdam 12 May 1928	COA	78: Columbia L 2182 78: Columbia (Italy) GQX 10942 78: Columbia (Holland) D 41003 78: Columbia (Japan) J 7319/JW 2826/ JW 425/W 299/C 8051 78: Columbia (USA) 67522D 78: Columbia (Argentina) AC 45 78: Odeon 0-8363/0-8381 78: Odeon (Australia) 0-4234 78: Odeon (Argentina) 177102 78: Decca (USA) 25484 LP: Columbia (Japan) KT 1-3 LP: Discocorp RR 421 LP: Pearl GEMM 212-213 CD: Pearl GEMMCDS 9070 CD: Music and Arts CD 809 Pearl CD edition contains both the original and an additional, previously unpublished, take

1812 Overture

Amsterdam 9 April 1940	COA	78: Telefunken SK 3080-3081 78: Telefunken (France) T 16-17 78: Ultraphon G 14271-14272 78: Supraphon G 22098-22099 78: Mercury 16017-16018/DM 23 78: Capitol 80084-80085/EBL 8022 45: Capitol KBM 8022 LP: Capitol L 8127 LP: Telefunken LB 6009 LP: Mercury MG 15000 LP: Metronome ULX 3009E LP: Past Masters PM 18 LP: Discocorp RR 443 CD: Teldec ZS 844.164/243.7302/ 4509 936732 CD: Dante LYS 175

MAX TRAPP (1887-1971)

Piano Concerto

Amsterdam 24 October 1935	COA Gieseking	Unpublished radio broadcast Recording incomplete

ANTONIO VIVALDI (1675-1741)

Concerto in A minor op 3 no 8

Amsterdam December 1937	COA	78: Telefunken SK 2401-2402 78: Telefunken (Japan) 23660-23661 78: Capitol 87006-87007/EBL 8057 45: Capitol KBM 8057 LP: Private issue (Japan) P 1001 CD: Archive Documents ADCD 112 CD: Biddulph WHL 024

ALEXANDER VORMOLEN (1895-1980)

Sinfonia

Amsterdam 31 October 1940	COA	LP: Past Masters PM 16

JOHANN WAGENAAR (1862-1941)

Cyrano de Bergerac, overture

Amsterdam April 1942	COA	78: Telefunken SK 3744-3745 LP: Past Masters PM 9 CD: Teldec ZS 844.157/243.7232

The Taming of the Shrew, overture

Amsterdam 10 October 1940	COA	LP: MRF Records MRF 74 CD: Donemus CVCD 7-10 CD: Colofon (Holland) COLOFON-4

RICHARD WAGNER (1813-1883)

Der fliegende Holländer, overture

Camden NJ 14 April 1924	NYPSO	Victor unpublished
Camden NJ 6 October 1925	NYPSO	78: Victor 6547 78: HMV D 1056/DB 905 78: HMV (France) W 734 78: Electrola EJ 575 CD: Biddulph WHL 025-026 CD: Pearl GEMMCDS 9922

Lohengrin, prelude

Amsterdam 10 June 1927	COA	78: Columbia L 1948 78: Columbia (Japan) J 7250 78: Odeon 0-8330 78: Odeon (France) 123532/123865 78: Odeon (Italy) N-6596 78: Odeon (Australia) 0-4069 78: Decca (USA) 25270 LP: Columbia (Japan) KT 1-3 CD: Pearl GEMMCDS 9018 CD: Symposium SYMCD 1078

Die Meistersinger von Nürnberg, overture

Amsterdam 12 November 1940	COA	78: Telefunken SK 3137 78: Telefunken (France) T 18 78: Capitol 80036 45: Capitol 80051 LP: Rococo 2012 LP: Discocorp RR 443 CD: Teldec ZS 844.162/243.7282

Siegfried, Forest murmurs

New York 14 December 1928	NYPSO	78: Victor 7192 78: Victor (Japan) JD 1570/ND 225 CD: Pearl GEMMCD 9474

Tristan und Isolde, Prelude and Liebestod

Amsterdam 23 November 1939	COA	LP: Archive Documents AD 103-104 CD: Archive Documents ADCD 116 CD: Seven Seas (Japan) KICC 2054 Seven Seas incorrectly dated 1943

GRAND-THÉATRE DE GENÈVE

ORCHESTRE DE LA SUISSE ROMANDE
ET ORCHESTRE RADIO-SUISSE-ROMANDE

Mercredi 27 février 1935, à 20 h. 30

8me CONCERT DE L'ABONNEMENT

sous la direction de Monsieur

WILLEM MENGELBERG

Chef d'orchestre du Concertgebouw d'Amsterdam

PROGRAMME :

1. **SYMPHONIE N° 6**, en fa majeur, **PASTORALE** . . . BEETHOVEN
   a) Allegro ma non troppo (Impressions heureuses à l'arrivée à la campagne) — b) Andante molto mosso (Au bord du ruisseau) — c) Allegro (Fête villageoise) - Allegro (Orage) — d) Allegretto (Chant des bergers - Sentiments de reconnaissance après l'orage).

2. **SINFONIA**, en si majeur . . . . J.-Chr. BACH
   Allegro assai - Andante - Presto.

3. **CIACONNA GOTHICA** (1re audition). . . . . Cornelius DOPPER

4. **LES PRÉLUDES**, poème symphonique. . . . F. LISZT

Location ouverte à l'Agence J. VÉRON, GRAUER & Cie, rue du Rhône, 27, à partir de Mardi 19 Février, de 9 heures à 12 h. 15 et de 13 h. 30 à 18 heures (le samedi jusqu'à 17 heures), Téléphone 41.254.

Tannhäuser, overture

Amsterdam May 1926	COA	78: Columbia L 1770-1771 78: Columbia (Italy) GQX 10328-10329 78: Columbia (Japan) J 7023-7024 78: Columbia (USA) 67221-67222D 78: Odeon O 8589-8590 78: Odeon (France) 86516-86517 78: Decca (USA) 25108-25109 LP: Columbia (Holland) 33HS 1003 CD: EMI CDH 769 9562 CD: Pearl GEMMCDS 9070
Amsterdam 9 May 1932	COA	78: Columbia LX 170-171 78: Columbia (Germany) LWX 18-19 78: Columbia (France) LFX 276-277 78: Columbia (Japan) J 8092-8093 78: Columbia (USA) X 27/MX 27 LP: Rococo 2012 LP: Discocorp RR 443 LP: EMI 5C 047 01298M CD: Pearl GEMMCDS 9018
Amsterdam 27 October 1940	COA	LP: Discocorp RR 234 CD: Music and Arts CD 780 CD: Seven Seas (Japan) KICC 2055

Die Walküre, Ride of the Valkyries

New York 4 January 1926	NYPSO	78: Brunswick 50161 78: Polydor (France) 595008 LP: Columbia (USA) BM 13/77224 CD: Pearl GEMMCDS 9922

CARL MARIA VON WEBER (1786-1826)

Euryanthe, overture

Amsterdam 1 June 1931	COA	78: Columbia LX 157 78: Columbia (Germany) LWX 326/DWX 1669 78: Columbia (France) LFX 249 78: Columbia (Italy) GQX 10994 78: Columbia (Japan) J 7964 78: Columbia (USA) 68069D CD: Pearl GEMMCDS 9018 CD: Dante LYS 089

Der Freischütz, overture

Amsterdam 1 June 1931	COA	78: Columbia LX 154 78: Columbia (Germany) LWX 325/DWX 1556 78: Columbia (Italy) GQX 10728 78: Columbia (USA) 68042D LP: Past Masters PM 4 CD: Pearl GEMMCDS 9018 CD: Dante LYS 089

Oberon, overture

Camden NJ 14 April 1922	NYPSO	78: Victor 74766-74767/6224 78: HMV DB 370 LP: Past Masters PM 6 CD: Biddulph WHL 025-026 CD: Symposium SYMCD 1078 CD: Dante LYS 089
Amsterdam 12 May 1928	COA	78: Columbia L 2312-2313/LCX 2-3 78: Columbia (France) LFX 317-318 78: Columbia (Holland) D 15840-15841 78: Columbia (Japan) J 7525-7526 78: Columbia (USA) X 34/MX 34 78: Odeon O 8397-8398/O 8373-8374 78: Odeon (Australia) O 4347-4348 78: Parlophone PX 01061-01062 78: Decca (USA) 25522-25523 LP: Discocorp RR 443 CD: Pearl GEMMCDS 9018 CD: Dante LYS 089
Paris 1931	COA	Unpublished video recording Filmed against backdrop of Concertgebouw Hall with spoken introduction by Mengelberg
Amsterdam 13 October 1940	COA	LP: Discocorp RR 234 CD: Music and Arts CD 780 CD: Seven Seas (Japan) KICC 2056

Oberon, excerpt (Ocean, thou mighty monster!)

Amsterdam 18 March 1943	COA Horna Sung in German	LP: Discocorp RR 234 CD: Archive Documents ADCD 109 CD: Seven Seas (Japan) KICC 2056 CD: Dante LYS 089

DUTCH NATIONAL ANTHEM

Amsterdam 2 June 1934	COA	Unpublished private recording Fragment also exists on film
Amsterdam 30 November 1938	COA	78: Telefunken A 2899 78: Telefunken (Holland) NK 1965 45: Telefunken (Holland) U 55220 LP: MRF Records MRF 74 LP: Past Masters PM 9 CD: Teldec ZS 844.157/243.7232

See also under composer Rudolf Mengelberg

INTERVIEWS

Mengelberg interviewed on his 40 years with the Concertgebouw Orchestra (1935)	CD: Archive Documents ADCD 109
Mengelberg speaks on the 50th anniversary of Concertgebouw Orchestra	CD: Archive Documents ADCD 109
Mengelberg interviewed in Munich in February 1938	Unpublished radio broadcast

Hermann Abendroth
1883-1956

Discography compiled
by John Hunt

FIRKET AMIROV (1922-1984)

Caucasian Sketches

Leipzig 1952	Leipzig RO	LP: Urania URLP 7117/US 57117 CD: Urania ULS 5156

JOHANN SEBASTIAN BACH (1685-1750)

Orchestral Suite No 3

Leipzig 20 September 1944	Gewandhaus Orchestra	CD: Tahra TAH 106-107
Leipzig 28 September 1949	Leipzig RO	LP: Eterna (Japan) ET 1511 CD: Eterna (Japan) 27TC-241 Air Eterna 120 116/25C-018

A recording of an unspecified Concerto for 3 pianos by Bach conducted by Abendroth may also survive

LUDWIG VAN BEETHOVEN (1770-1827)

Symphony No 1

Date not confirmed	Leipzig RO	78: Eterna 26.47-49/321.007-009

Symphony No 1, First movement

Berlin 1922	BPO	78: Grammophon 65874

Symphony No 3 "Eroica"

Berlin 31 March 1952	East Berlin RO	Unpublished radio broadcast Fourth movement CD: Melodram MEL 18020 Melodram incorrectly dated March 1950
Berlin 13 February 1954	East Berlin RO	CD: Tahra TAH 129-131

German newsreel film exists of Abendroth conducting the opening bars of the Eroica in Berlin

Symphony No 4

Leipzig 4 December 1949	Leipzig RO	LP: Urania URRS 717 LP: Music Treasures of the World MT 49 LP: Eterna (Japan) ET 1503 LP: Melodiya M10 44957 CD: Arlecchino ARL 75 CD: Tahra TAH 183-184 Rehearsal extract CD: Tahra TAH 102

Symphony No 5

Berlin 1939	BPO	78: Odeon O 7898-7901 78: Parlophone E 11434-11437 CD: Tahra TAH 102

Symphony No 6 "Pastoral"

Leipzig 18 June 1950	Leipzig RO	LP: Eterna (Japan) ET 1501 CD: Arlecchino ARL 75 Arlecchino incorrectly dated 1949

Symphony No 9 "Choral"

Leipzig 23 March 1939	Gewandhaus Orchestra and Chorus Lehrergesangverein Briem, Hennecke, W.Ludwig, Watzke	Unpublished radio broadcast
Stockholm 7 April 1943	Stockholm PO and Chorus Soloists	CD: Tahra awaiting publication Final movement bars 647-729 CD: Bis BISCD 421-424
Berlin December 1950	East Berlin RO and Chorus Briem, Eustrati, Suthaus, Paul	Unpublished radio broadcast
Prague 9 June 1951	Czech PO and Chorus Stouchkova, Linhartova, Blachut, Haken Sung in Czech	CD: Tahra TAH 129-131 Short extract from this performance also exists on unpublished video recording
Leipzig June 1951	Leipzig RO and Chorus Schlemm, Eustrati, Lutze, Paul	78: Ultraphon H 24006-24014 LP: Supraphon LPM 48-50/5048-5050/ MM 132-137/SUA 130 255-130 256/ SUA 10 255-10 256/EF 302/DV 5294/ LPV 218-219/BLPV 218-219 CD: Arlecchino ARL 150
Leipzig 29 June 1951	Leipzig RO and Chorus Laux, Eustrati, Suthaus, Paul	78: Eterna E26.1-9 LP: Urania URSP 101 LP: Music Treasures of the World MT 11/MT 211 LP: Eterna 822 175-822 176 LP: Eterna (Japan) ET1012/ET1502-1503 CD: Eterna (Japan) 32TC-113 CD: Urania ULS 5160 CD: Arlecchino ARL 74

Piano Concerto No 4

Date not confirmed	BPO Kempff	CD: Tahra awaiting publication
Date not confirmed	East Berlin RO Then-Bergh	CD: Tahra TAH 212

Piano Concerto No 5 "Emperor"

Berlin 13 October 1944	BPO Ney	CD: Tahra TAH 192-193

Violin Concerto

Berlin 31 March 1952	East Berlin RO Oistrakh	LP: Melodiya M10 46361 CD: Melodram MEL 18020 CD: Pilz 78000 CD: Arlecchino ARL 164 CD: Tahra TAH 129-131 Melodram and Arlecchino incorrectly dated 1950; rehearsal extract from this performance also exists as unpublished video recording

Violin Romance No 1

Berlin 31 March 1952	East Berlin RO Oistrakh	CD: Melodram MEL 18020 CD: Tahra TAH 129-131 Melodram incorrectly dated 1950

Violin Romance No 2

Berlin 31 March 1952	East Berlin RO Oistrakh	Unpublished radio broadcast Tape cannot be traced

Coriolan overture

Leipzig 27 May 1949	Leipzig RO	CD: Tahra TAH 129-131

Egmont overture

Berlin 13 February 1954	East Berlin RO	LP: Melodiya M10 44957 CD: Melodram MEL 18020 CD: Pilz 78000 CD: Tahra TAH 129-131 Melodram incorrectly dated 1950; Melodiya and Pilz dated 1952

Fidelio overture

Berlin 1939	BPO	78: Odeon 0-4617 78: Odeon (France) 0-188100 CD: Tahra awaiting publication

Leonore No 3 overture

Date not confirmed	Leipzig RO	LP: Melodiya D 4056-4057 CD: Tahra TAH 183-184

JOHANNES BRAHMS (1833-1897)

Symphony No 1

London 1928	LSO	78: HMV D 1454-1458 78: HMV (Austria) ES 276-281 CD: Tahra TAH 145-146
Berlin 3-29 July 1941	BPO	78: Odeon O 9122-9127 CD: Tahra TAH 102
Date not confirmed	Leipzig RO	78: Ultraphon H 24249-24245 LP: Ultraphon 50549 LP: Supraphon DV 5045/LPV 69/ LPVE 10158
Leipzig 20 October 1949	Leipzig RO	78: Eterna 26.10-15 LP: Eterna (Japan) ET 1504 CD: Eterna (Japan) 27TC-232 CD: Arlecchino ARL 162
Munich 16 January 1956	Bavarian State Orchestra	CD: Tahra TAH 141-142

Symphony No 2

Date not confirmed	Leipzig RO	78: Ultraphon H 24059-24063 LP: Ultraphon 50439 LP: Supraphon LPV 56 CD: Arlecchino ARL 130

Philharmonisches Orchester G. m. b. H., Berlin W 35, Dörnbergstr. 6

Bernburger Str. 22 **PHILHARMONIE** Bernburger Str. 22

Sonntag, den 5. April 1936, vormittags 11½ Uhr
Montag, den 6. April 1936, abends 8 Uhr

9. Philharmonisches Konzert

Leitung:

Hermann Abendroth

Solistin: Elly Ney

BRAHMS-ABEND

I. Tragische Ouvertüre d-moll, op. 81

II. Konzert für Klavier mit Orchester Nr. 2 B-dur, op. 83
Allegro non troppo
Allegro appassionato
Andante
Allegretto grazioso

Elly Ney

— Pause —

III. Sinfonie Nr. 4 e-moll, op. 98
Allegro non troppo
Andante moderato
Allegro grazioso (Intermezzo)
Allegro energico e passionato (Ciacona)

Konzertflügel 

BECHSTEIN

PHILHARMONIE, Montag, 20. April 1936, abends 8 Uhr
10. PHILHARMONISCHES KONZERT
Leitung: WILHELM FURTWÄNGLER
Solisten: Wilhelm Furtwängler, Hugo Kolberg, Albert Harzer
Öffentliche Voraufführung: Sonntag, den 19. April 1936, vormittags 11½ Uhr

QUEEN'S HALL, Langham Place, W.1.

Sole Lessees - - - - Messrs. CHAPPELL & Co., LTD.

LONDON SYMPHONY ORCHESTRA

1929	ARTISTS.	CONDUCTORS.
Dec. 9	**DORFMANN**	**BARBIROLLI**
1930		
Jan. 20	**KREISLER**	**ABENDROTH**
Feb. 10	**Wagner Programme AUSTRAL and WIDDOP**	**ALBERT COATES**
Mar. 10	**CORTOT**	**ABENDROTH**
Mar. 24		**Dr. FELIX WEINGARTNER**
Apr. 7		**Dr. FELIX WEINGARTNER**

SINGLE TICKETS (*including Tax*)

Stalls	17/-, 12/-, 8/6	December 9th, February 10th, March 10th, March 24th, April 7th
Grand Circle	17/-, 12/-	
Balcony	5/9	
Orchestra	4/9	
Area	3/6	

SINGLE TICKETS (*including Tax*)

Stalls	17/-, 12/-, 8/6	January 20th (KREISLER)
Grand Circle	17/-, 12/-	
Balcony	10/6	
Orchestra	5/9	
Area	5/9	

Tickets can be obtained at CHAPPELL'S BOX OFFICE QUEEN'S HALL (open 10 a.m. to 6 p.m. and 50, New Bond Street, W.; the usual Agents and Libraries, and of

LIONEL POWELL, 161, New Bond Street, W.1
Telephone: REGENT 1204. 5, 6 and 7.

(Stamped and addressed envelopes with all enquiries.)

Symphony No 3

Prague 1951	Czech PO	CD: Arlecchino ARL 71
Date not confirmed	Prague RO	78: Ultraphon H 23978-23982 LP: Ultraphon 50449 LP: Supraphon LPV 57/K 203162/ SUA 10206 LP: Discophile (Italy) 3029 CD: Arlecchino ARL 162
Leipzig 17 March 1952	Leipzig RO	LP: Urania URRS 75 LP: Music Treasures of the World MT 547 LP: American Recording Society MP 26 LP: Classics Club MP 26 LP: Lyrique HP 1005 LP: Eterna 820 006 LP: Eterna (Japan) ET 1505 CD: Eterna (Japan) 27TC-233 CD: Arlecchino ARL 108 Arlecchino dated 1949

Symphony No 4

London March 1927	LSO	78: HMV D 1265-1270 78: Victor M 31/G 7 CD: Tahra TAH 102
Leipzig 27-28 June 1942	Gewandhaus Orchestra	78: Odeon O 9142-9147 CD: Tahra awaiting publication
Leipzig 8 December 1954	Leipzig RO	LP: Eterna 820 007 LP: Eterna (Japan) ET 1506 CD: Eterna (Japan) 27TC-234 CD: Arlecchino ARL 127

Serenade No 1

Date not confirmed	Leipzig RO	CD: Tahra TAH 145-146

Violin Concerto

Date not confirmed	Leipzig RO Manke	LP: Urania URS 724 LP: Music Treasures of the World MT 550
Berlin March 1952	East Berlin RO Oistrakh	CD: Tahra awaiting publication

Double Concerto

Date not confirmed	Leipzig RO Kirmse, Günther	CD: Tahra TAH 145-146

Ein deutsches Requiem

Berlin November 1952	East Berlin RO and Chorus Schmidt-Glänzel Friedrich	CD: Arlecchino ARL 92

Haydn Variations

Leipzig 19 December 1949	Leipzig RO	LP: Eterna (Japan) ET 1505 CD: Eterna (Japan) 27TC-233 CD: Arlecchino ARL 71 Arlecchino dated 1952

Tragic overture

Leipzig 26 March 1945	Gewandhaus Orchestra	CD: Arlecchino ARL 71

MAX BRUCH (1838-1920)

Violin Concerto No 1

Berlin 16 December 1944	BPO Taschner	CD: Tahra TAH 192-193

ANTON BRUCKNER (1824-1896)

Symphony No 4 "Romantic"

Leipzig 16 November 1949	Leipzig RO	LP: Urania URLP 401 LP: Eterna (Japan) ET 1023/ET 1518 CD: Eterna (Japan) 27TC-244 CD: Berlin Classics BC 92772 CD: Arlecchino ARL 107 Arlecchino dated 1951

Symphony No 5

Leipzig 27 May 1949	Leipzig RO	LP: Eterna (Japan) ET 1024-1025/ ET 1519-1520 CD: Eterna (Japan) 27TC-245 CD: Berlin Classics BC 92802 CD: Arlecchino ARL 149

Symphony No 7

Berlin 16-17 February 1956	East Berlin RO	CD: Tahra TAH 114-115

Symphony No 8

Leipzig 28 September 1949	Leipzig RO	CD: Tahra TAH 114-115

Symphony No 9

Leipzig 29 October 1951	Leipzig RO	LP: Eterna (Japan) ET 1026/ET 1521 CD: Eterna (Japan) 27TC-246 CD: Berlin Classics BC 20502/BC 91112

FREDERIC CHOPIN (1810-1849)

Piano Concerto No 2, Second movement

Leipzig 5 May 1952	Leipzig RO Sztompka	LP: Muza (Poland) SX 2015-2016

ERNST VON DOHNANYI (1877-1960)

Wedding waltz (The Veil of Pierrette)

Berlin 1938	Staatskapelle	78: Odeon 0-4570 78: Parlophone A 6945/R 2486/DPW 52

ANTONIN DVORAK (1841-1904)

Cello Concerto

Leipzig 28 March 1956	Leipzig RO Hoelscher	LP: Eterna 821 926 LP: Eterna (Japan) ET 1021/ET 1516 CD: Eterna (Japan) 27TC-242 CD: Arlecchino ARL 185

HANNS EISLER (1898-1962)

Rhapsodie für grosses Orchester

Date not confirmed	Leipzig RO	78: Eterna 28.32-33

CHRISTOPH WILLIBALD GLUCK (1714-1787)

Iphigenie in Aulis, overture

Berlin 1939	Staatskapelle	78: Odeon 0-7894 78: Parlophone A 4550/E 11446
Berlin 21 September 1944	BPO	LP: Urania URLP 7028 LP: Music Treasures of the World MT 501 CD: Arlecchino ARL 93 CD: Tahra TAH 139-140

Orfeo ed Euridice, excerpt (Che farò)

Berlin 21 September 1944	BPO Klose Sung in German	CD: Tahra TAH 192-193

Orfeo ed Euridice, Dance of the furies & Dance of the blessed spirits

Berlin 21 September 1944	BPO	CD: Tahra TAH 192-193

PAUL GRAENER (1872-1944)

Comedietta

Berlin 1939	Staatskapelle	78: Odeon 0-7912

GEORGE FRIDERIC HANDEL (1685-1759)

Concerto grosso op 6 no 5, Second and fifth movements

Cologne 14 January 1933	Cologne CO	78: Odeon O-11833 78: Parlophone A 6045/R 1933 78: Decca (USA) 20044 78: Gramophone (Czechoslovakia) 17035D CD: Tahra TAH 102

Concerto grosso op 6 no 6

Berlin 20 September 1944	BPO	CD: Tahra TAH 192-193
Leipzig 24 October 1944	Gewandhaus Orchestra	CD: Tahra TAH 106-107

Concerto grosso op 6 no 10, Second and sixth movements

Cologne 14 January 1933	Cologne CO	78: Odeon O-11852 78: Parlophone R 1934 78: Decca (USA) 20045 CD: Tahra TAH 102

Concerto a due cori No 3 in F

Berlin 15 September 1955	East Berlin RO	LP: Eterna (Japan) ET 1511 CD: Eterna (Japan) 27TC-242

Giulio Cesare, excerpt (V'adoro pupille)

Berlin 21 September 1944	BPO Klose Sung in German	LP: Eterna 820 922 CD: Tahra TAH 192-193

FRANZ JOSEF HAYDN (1732-1809)

Symphony No 88

Leipzig 10 October 1944	Gewandhaus Orchestra	LP: Eterna 827 453 CD: Arlecchino ARL 86 CD: Tahra TAH 106-107 Arlecchino incorrectly dated 1950
Leipzig 1956	Leipzig RO	LP: Eterna 820 047 LP: Eterna (Japan) ET 1017/ET 1510 CD: Eterna (Japan) 27TC-237 CD: Berlin Classics 92862

Symphony No 96 "Miracle"

Leipzig 10 January 1945	Gewandhaus Orchestra	CD: Arlecchino ARL 86 CD: Tahra TAH 106-107

Symphony No 97

Berlin January 1955	East Berlin RO	LP: Eterna 820 047 LP: Eterna (Japan) ET 1017/ET 1510 CD: Eterna (Japan) 27TC-237 CD: Arlecchino ARL 86 CD: Berlin Classics 92862 Arlecchino incorrectly described as Leipzig 1950

Symphony No 103 "Drum Roll"

Leipzig 29 October 1951	Leipzig RO	CD: Tahra TAH 139-140

ENGELBERT HUMPERDINCK (1854-1921)

Maurische Rhapsodie

Leipzig 1944-1945	Gewandhaus Orchestra	LP: Urania URLP 7020 LP: Classics Club X 1047 LP: Avon AVS 13017 CD: Arlecchino ARL 128

BASIL KALINNIKOV (1866-1901)

Symphony No 1

Leipzig 16 November 1949	Leipzig RO	CD: Tahra TAH 141-142

FRANZ LISZT (1811-1886)

Hungarian Rhapsody No 1

Berlin 19 June 1937	Staatskapelle	78: Odeon 0-7734 78: Odeon (France) 0-170158 78: Parlophone E 11334

Hungarian Rhapsody No 4

Berlin 1 October 1938	BPO	78: Odeon 0-7887 78: Parlophone E 11389 CD: Tahra awaiting publication

FELIX MENDELSSOHN-BARTHOLDY (1809-1847)

Hebrides, overture

Leipzig 18 September 1949	Leipzig RO	CD: Arlecchino ARL 93 CD: Tahra TAH 139-140

A Midsummer Night's Dream, overture

Leipzig 13 August 1950	Leipzig RO	CD: Tahra TAH 139-140

MODEST MOUSSORGSKY (1835-1881)

Pictures from an exhibition, arranged by Ravel

Date not confirmed	Leipzig RO	LP: Urania URLP 7157/URRS 718 LP: Music Treasures of the World MT 37/MT 521 CD: Arlecchino ARL 128

WOLFGANG AMADEUS MOZART (1756-1791)

Symphony No 29

Leipzig 10 October 1944	Gewandhaus Orchestra	CD: Arlecchino ARL 7 CD: Tahra TAH 106-107

Symphony No 33

Leipzig 9 January 1956	Leipzig RO	CD: Arlecchino ARL 163 CD: Berlin Classics BC 92712

Symphony No 35 "Haffner"

Berlin 16 September 1956	East Berlin RO	LP: Eterna (Japan) ET 1507 CD: Eterna (Japan) 27TC-235 CD: Arlecchino ARL 163 CD: Berlin Classics BC 92712

Symphony No 38 "Prague"

Berlin 16 February 1955	East Berlin RO	LP: Eterna 821 634 LP: Eterna (Japan) ET 1708 CD: Eterna (Japan) 27TC-235 CD: Berlin Classics BC 92712

Symphony No 39

Leipzig 9 February 1953	Leipzig RO	CD: Tahra TAH 139-140

Symphony No 41 "Jupiter"

Leipzig 26 March 1956	Leipzig RO	LP: Eterna 821 634 LP: Eterna (Japan) ET 1509 CD: Eterna (Japan) 27TC-236 CD: Arlecchino ARL 7 CD: Berlin Classics BC 92712 Arlecchino incorrectly dated 1952

Piano Concerto No 27

Date not confirmed	East Berlin RO Then-Bergh	CD: Tahra TAH 212

Violin Concerto No 3

Berlin 21 September 1944	BPO Röhn	CD: Tahra TAH 192-193

Divertimento No 7

Leipzig 26 March 1956	Leipzig RO	LP: Eterna (Japan) ET 1509 CD: Eterna (Japan) 27TC-236 CD: Arlecchino ARL 7 CD: Berlin Classics BC 92712 Berlin Classics incorrectly describe orchestra as Leipzig Gewandhaus

Serenade No 6 "Serenata notturna", Second and third movements

Cologne 14 January 1933	Cologne CO	78: Odeon O-11805 78: Parlophone R 1905 78: Decca (USA) 20109 CD: Tahra TAH 102

Serenade No 8

Berlin 12 April 1956	East Berlin RO	LP: Eterna (Japan) ET 1508 CD: Eterna (Japan) 27TC-236 CD: Berlin Classics BC 92712

HANS PFITZNER (1869-1949)

Symphony No 2 "Kleine Sinfonie"

Leipzig 1944-1945	Gewandhaus Orchestra	LP: Urania URLP 7044

GABRIEL POPOV (1904-1972)

Symphony No 2 "Patria"

Date not confirmed	Leipzig RO	LP: Urania URLP 7163 CD: Urania ULS 5156 WERM incorrectly describes orchestra as LPO

GIACOMO PUCCINI (1858-1924)

Madama Butterfly, orchestral potpourri

Berlin 1938	BPO	78: Parlophone E 11369

MAX REGER (1873-1916)

Variations on a theme of Mozart, omitting final fugue

Paris 9 December 1941	Conservatoire Orchestra	78: HMV DB 5197-5198 CD: Tahra awaiting publication

Eine Böcklin-Suite

Date not confirmed		CD: Tahra TAH 183-184

FRANZ SCHUBERT (1797-1828)

Symphony No 3

Leipzig 19 February 1945	Gewandhaus Orchestra	CD: Arlecchino ARL 192 CD: Tahra TAH 106-107

Symphony No 8 "Unfinished"

Leipzig 18 September 1949	Leipzig RO	LP: Eterna 822 176 LP: Eterna (Japan) ED 2/ET 1027 CD: Eterna (Japan) 27TC-238 CD: Arlecchino ARL 176 CD: Berlin Classics BC 20512/BC 91112 Arlecchino incorrectly dated 1950
Budapest December 1955	Hungarian State Orchestra	Unpublished radio broadcast

Symphony No 9 "Great"

Leipzig 11 January 1950	Leipzig RO	LP: Eterna 821 635 LP: Eterna (Japan) ET 1018/ET 1512 CD: Eterna (Japan) 27TC-238 CD: Berlin Classics BC 20512/BC 91112
Berlin 29 September 1955	East Berlin RO	CD: Tahra TAH 139-140

ROBERT SCHUMANN (1810-1856)

Symphony No 1 "Spring"

Berlin 18 September 1955	East Berlin RO	CD: Tahra TAH 141-142

Symphony No 2

Date not confirmed	Leipzig RO	CD: Arlecchino ARL 94

Symphony No 4

Leipzig 31 March 1956	Leipzig RO	LP: Eterna 720 015 LP: Eterna (Japan) ED 2/ET 1020 CD: Eterna (Japan) 27TC-239 CD: Arlecchino ARL 94 CD: Berlin Classics BC 20532/BC 91112

Piano Concerto

Berlin 13 March 1956	East Berlin RO Wührer	LP: Eterna 821 955 LP: Eterna (Japan) ET 1022/ET 1517 CD: Eterna (Japan) 27TC-243 CD: Arlecchino ARL 164 CD: Berlin Classics BC 20522/BC 91112

Cello Concerto

Leipzig 3 September 1955	Leipzig RO Tortelier	LP: Eterna 821 955 LP: Eterna (Japan) ET 1022/ET 1517 CD: Eterna (Japan) 27TC-243 CD: Arlecchino ARL 185 CD: Berlin Classics BC 20522/BC 91112

Manfred overture

Leipzig 28 December 1944	Gewandhaus Orchestra	45: Urania UREP 45 LP: Urania URRS 719 CD: Arlecchino ARL 94 CD: Tahra TAH 106-107 Arlecchino incorrectly describes orchestra as Leipzig RO

FÜNFZEHNTES

GEWANDHAUS-KONZERT

DONNERSTAG, 27. FEBRUAR 1941, 6 UHR

Dirigent: *Hermann Abendroth*

*

Von deutscher Seele

Eine romantische Kantate
nach Sprüchen und Gedichten von Joseph von Eichendorff
für vier Solostimmen, gemischten Chor, großes Orchester und Orgel (op. 28)

von HANS PFITZNER (geb. 1869)

1. Teil: Mensch und Natur
2. Teil: Leben und Singen

Soli: *Marta Schilling, Gertrude Pitzinger*
Heinz Marten, Fred Drissen
Orgel: *Sigfrid Walther Müller*

Pause nach dem ersten Teil **Ende des Konzertes 8 Uhr**

Text in besonderem Heft Klavierauszüge sind im Erdgeschoß erhältlich

GEWANDHAUS ZU LEIPZIG

FÜNFTES

GEWANDHAUS-KONZERT

DONNERSTAG, 29. NOVEMBER 1945, 18.30 UHR

IM „CAPITOL“

Dirigent: *Hermann Abendroth*

★

ROBERT SCHUMANN (1810–1856)

Ouvertüre zu Byrons „Manfred“ (op. 115)

ANTON BRUCKNER (1824–1896)

Symphonie Nr. 7, E-dur

I. Allegro moderato.

II. Adagio. Sehr feierlich und langsam.

III. Scherzo. Sehr schnell.

IV. Bewegt, doch nicht schnell.

Erläuterungen umseitig

1. GEWANDHAUS-KAMMERMUSIK: Sonntag, den 9. Dezember, 10 Uhr im „Capitol“: Tschaikowsky: Streichquartett D-dur, op. 11. Mozart, Klarinettenquintett. Gewandhaus-Quartett und Willy Schreinicke (Klarinette).

6. GEWANDHAUS-KONZERT: Donnerstag, den 20. Dezember, 18.30 Uhr, Hauptprobe 9.30 Uhr im „Capitol“. Dirigent: Hermann Abendroth. Werke von Ludwig van Beethoven (im Gedenken an Beethovens 175. Geburtstag am 16. Dezember). Prometheus-Musik, Szene und Arie „Ah perfido“ (Gesang: Gertrud Bäumer), Ouvertüre zu „Leonore“ Nr. 3, IV. Symphonie, B-dur.

JEAN SIBELIUS (1865-1957)

Symphony No 2

Leipzig 1951	Leipzig RO	LP: Urania URLP 7145 LP: Classics Club X 131 LP: Music Treasures of the World MT 514 CD: Arlecchino ARL 108

Finlandia

Berlin 1938	BPO	78: Odeon 0-7896 78: Parlophone E 11418 78: Columbia (Japan) J 8700

JOHANN STRAUSS (1825-1899)

An der schönen blauen Donau, waltz

Leipzig 18 November 1950	Leipzig RO	45: Urania UREP 45 LP: Urania URLP 7115/URRS 721 LP: World Records CMD 315 CD: Arlecchino ARLA 17 CD: Tahra TAH 141-142

Die Fledermaus, overture

Berlin 1922	BPO	78: Grammophon 65870

A version of the overture on Urania, World Records and Arlecchino and attributed to Leipzig RO/Abendroth appears to be a performance by VPO/Böhm

Kaiserwalzer

Leipzig 18 November 1950	Leipzig RO	CD: Tahra TAH 141-142

Waldmeister, overture

Leipzig 18 November 1950	Leipzig RO	45: Urania UREP 60 LP: Urania URLP 7115/URRS 721 LP: World Records CMD 315 CD: Arlecchino ARLA 17 CD: Tahra TAH 141-142

Wiener Blut, waltz

Berlin 1922	BPO	78: Grammophon 65875/69252

Der Zigeunerbaron, overture

Leipzig 18 November 1950	Leipzig RO	45: Urania UREP 54 LP: Urania URLP 7115/URRS 721 LP: World Records CMD 315 CD: Arlecchino ARLA 17 CD: Tahra TAH 141-142

Versions of Künstlerleben and Frühlingsstimmen waltzes on Urania, World Records and Arlecchino and attributed to Leipzig RO/Abendroth, appear to be performances by Leipzig RO/Kegel

RICHARD STRAUSS (1864-1949)

Don Juan

Leipzig 11 February 1952	Leipzig RO	CD: Tahra TAH 138

Don Quixote

Berlin 22 January 1955	East Berlin RO Danyi	LP: Eterna (Japan) ET 1515 CD: Eterna (Japan) 27TC-241

Till Eulenspiegels lustige Streiche

Leipzig 14 November 1950	Leipzig RO	CD: Tahra TAH 138

Tod und Verklärung

Berlin 1922	BPO	78: Grammophon 65871-65873
Leipzig 24 October 1949	Leipzig RO	CD: Tahra TAH 138

PIOTR TCHAIKOVSKY (1840-1893)

Symphony No 4

Leipzig 13 February 1951	Leipzig RO	LP: Urania URLP 7159/URRS 725 LP: Eterna 822 178 LP: Saga XID 5239 LP: Eterna (Japan) ET 1019/ET 1513 CD: Eterna (Japan) 27TC-239 CD: Arlecchino ARL 64 CD: Berlin Classics BC 20532/BC 91112 Third movement 45: Urania UREP 61 Saga edition incorrectly describes orchestra as Leipzig Gewandhaus

Symphony No 6 "Pathétique"

Leipzig 28 January 1951	Leipzig RO	LP: Urania URLP 7147/URRS 712 LP: Music Treasures of the World MTW 29 LP: Classics Club M 29 LP: Eterna (Japan) ET 1020/ET 1514 CD: Eterna (Japan) 27TC-240 CD: Berlin Classics BC 20542/BC 91112 Berlin Classics dated January 1952

Violin Concerto

Date not confirmed	Leipzig RO Schulz	LP: Urania URRS 77 CD: Arlecchino ARL 64

Orchestral Suite No 3

Date not confirmed		CD: Tahra TAH 183-184

MAX TRAPP (1887-1971)

Symphony No 2

Berlin September- December 1944	BPO	Unpublished radio broadcast

ANTONIO VIVALDI (1675-1741)

Concerto op 3 no 8, First and second movements

Cologne 14 January 1933	Cologne CO	78: Odeon 0-11813 78: Odeon (Spain) 0-203444 78: Parlophone R 1996 78: Decca (USA) 20042 CD: Tahra TAH 102

RICHARD WAGNER (1813-1883)

A Faust overture

Berlin 22 September 1944	BPO	CD: Radio Years RY 66-67

Der fliegende Holländer, overture

Berlin 1 October 1938	BPO	78: Odeon 0-7888 78: Odeon (Brazil) C 7313 78: Parlophone E 11422 78: Columbia (Japan) JW 699 LP: EMI RLS 768 CD: EMI CDF 300 0122 CD: Tahra awaiting publication

Die Meistersinger von Nürnberg

Bayreuth July 1943	Bayreuth Festival Orchestra & Chorus Scheppan, Kallab, Suthaus, Witte, Schöffler, Dalberg, Krenn, Kunz, Pina	CD: Preiser 90174 <u>Excerpts</u> LP: Acanta HB 22863/40.23502 CD: Preiser 90325 CD: Arlecchino ARL 93

Tannhäuser, excerpt (O du mein holder Abendstern)

Budapest December 1955	Hungarian State Orchestra S.Sved	LP: Hungaroton HLPMK 1503

Die Walküre, excerpt (Leb' wohl, du kühnes herrliches Kind!)

Budapest December 1955	Hungarian State Orchestra S.Sved	LP: Hungaroton HLX 90039/LPX 12094 CD: Arlecchino ARL 93

Wesendonk-Lieder

Leipzig 1950	Leipzig RO Lemnitz	CD: Arlecchino ARL 93

CARL MARIA VON WEBER (1786-1826)

Der Freischütz, overture

Budapest December 1955	Hungarian State Orchestra	CD: Arlecchino ARL 93

Oberon, overture

Munich 16 January 1956	Bavarian State Orchestra	CD: Tahra TAH 139-140

HERMANN ABENDROTH SPEAKS

Tahra proposes to publish various recorded interviews: the first of these has been published on CD TAH 192-193.

A POSTSCRIPT BY BILL FLOWERS

Hermann Abendroth - the demon Kapellmeister

Matthew Arnold said that England was the only country in Europe where the word culture has a slightly pejorative ring. The same might be said for the term Kapellmeister. It tends to conjure up a vision of a solid, worthy, reliable but rather unexciting routinier.

Was Hermann Abendroth a Kapellmeister? Well, he certainly seems to have started out as one, judging by his recordings of Brahms 1 and 4 with the LSO and issued by HMV in 1927-1928. Rather easy-going and placid are the terms that spring to mind. What changed him then? Was it the example of his more romantic and subjective contemporaries, Mengelberg and Furtwängler, or maybe the trauma of the Hitler years and World War II? Was it perhaps that "old man's frenzy" of which the poet W.B.Yeats speaks?

Whatever the reason, there are times when one can hardly believe that some of his wartime and post-war recordings are by the same artist. In Brahms and Schubert tempo changes are now abrupt and violent, sometimes shockingly so, to the extent that they completely undermine the structure of the music. All this is combined with savage fortissimos and thunderous tympani. Certainly no one would dare play Brahms like this today. Perhaps it was all due to a personality change, for by all accounts Abendroth became increasingly arrogant and unpredictable as he grew older.

In the last year of the war, when the RAF were venting their own version of the holocaust on German cities, Abendroth and the Leipzig Gewandhaus were, amid all the carnage, producing performances of a quite astonishing beauty and intensity: a sort of affirmation of the light against the forces of barbarism which were about to engulf Germany.

After the war Abendroth remained in what was soon to become the German Democratic Republic, assiduously courted by the communist authorities. He also became quite peripatetic, by his standards at least. He had never been much given to travelling, and long years in Cologne and Leipzig, with few guest engagements abroad, had no doubt contributed to his reputation as a sound and reliable provincial performer rather than an international superstar. But now he found himself in demand all over the Eastern bloc. In the closely guarded and beleaguered half-country that was East Germany, Abendroth became (along with Bertolt Brecht) their chief cultural icon. Personal friendship with Dictator Ulbricht ensured him luxuries and limousines in that austere and autocratic state but hardly endeared him to the authorities in Bonn.

Hermann Abendroth was the very first German musician to be invited to the Soviet Union after the war. Filled with some trepidation concerning his reception, he set out for Moscow in 1951. After a bumpy 6½-hour flight in a piston-engined Ilyushin he found himself welcomed with speeches and bouquets and accorded a motorcade to the Kremlin. PR soon gave way to artistic triumphs as he travelled from city to city. Two months later he was welcomed back to East Berlin by Ulbricht in person, and presented with the Order of Karl Marx, the GDR's highest decoration.

From 1948 Abendroth was not only music director of the Weimar State Theatre but also chief guest conductor of the Leipzig Gewandhaus and East Berlin Radio Orchestras. But he now seemed to be ignored, one might almost say ostracised, in the West. One could read "Gramophone" for a year and not come across his name. This made it very difficult for his small group of admirers west of the iron curtain to assemble a collection of his recordings, which had not been all that numerous anyway. Fortunately he seemed to have a considerable following in Japan, and it was here that a large part of his repertoire was issued on superbly engineered Eterna LPs.

If Abendroth thought of himself as a big fish in a small pond, it did seem by the mid 1950s that he was breaking free from his somewhat constricted milieu. He was booked for 1957 for long tours of South America and Japan, but his sudden death from a stroke in the spring of 1956 put an end to these plans. He was accorded one of those huge, pompous state funerals so beloved of dictatorships whether of the left or right. But he had been truly loved and revered in Weimar and Leipzig, and huge crowds lined the streets. Although Abendroth has had successors of the calibre of Konwitschny and Masur, no one in the eyes of those cities has ever quite succeeded in taking his place.

For many years in Britain we hardly heard of Hermann Abendroth. Suddenly the tide turned and now both Arlecchino and Tahra are re-issuing not only his much sought after but rather slender legacy of studio recordings, but off-the-air radio performances and live concerts as well. Now the trickle of CDs has become a flood and one no longer has to browse through the basements of specialist LP dealers to build up a comprehensive collection of his recordings.

And treasures there are indeed to be had! Some may be too wayward and eccentric for any but the most fanatical devotee, but others are quite unmissable. That legendary wartime "Meistersinger" from Bayreuth and the incredible Beethoven 9 with the Czech Philharmonic from the 1951 Prague Festival, played with a frenzied intensity which rivals Furtwängler's 1942 performance. This truly apocalyptic version, only recently come to light and issued by Tahra (TAH 129-131) must be heard to be believed. Abendroth was also a wonderful conductor of Richard Strauss: Michael Tanner considers his "Don Juan" the most fiery and impetuous he has ever heard. And there is a Tchaikovsky "Pathétique" quite frightening in its intensity.

Nowadays authenticity and moderation are the order of the day, so the chances are that you will never hear the Choral Symphony played like this again. Michael Tanner also asked if people can really prefer our current gurus of the podium, with their impeccably safe performances, to this apocalyptic music-making. Seemingly, God help us, some of those people can!

As for Hermann Abendroth, if he was indeed a Kapellmeister once, he certainly broke the mould and left us some of the most exciting and extraordinary performances ever put on record.

Dimitri Mitropoulos
1896-1960

with valuable assistance from Stathis Arfanis

Discography compiled
by John Hunt

JOHANN SEBASTIAN BACH (1685-1750)

Brandenburg Concerto No 5

New York 16 December 1945	NBC SO Mitropoulos, piano	CD: As-Disc AS 512 CD: Discantus (Greece) 189 6212

Orchestral Suite No 3

New York 18 April 1954	NYPSO	Unpublished radio broadcast

Concerto in D minor

Salzburg 10 August 1958	Concertgebouw Orchestra Gould	LP: Discocorp IGI 206 CD: Nuova era 013.6306 CD: Priceless D 15119 CD: Memories HR 4415-4416 CD: NAS 6204 CD: Discantus (Greece) 189 6282

Concerto in F minor

New York 18 December 1949	NYPSO Szigeti	LP: Rococo 2037 LP: Discocorp RR 532 LP: Melodiya D 092257 CD: As-Disc AS 626 CD: Music and Arts CD 668 CD: Discantus (Greece) 189 6282

Concerto in D minor for 3 pianos

New York 27 November 1950	NYPSO Robert, Gaby and Jean Casadesus	LP: Columbia (USA) ML 2196 LP: Philips A01620R/S06695R

Chaconne from Violin Partia in D minor, arranged by Casella

Turin May 1950	RAI Torino Orchestra	LP: Cetra LPC 50044 CD: Nickson NN 1003 CD: Discantus (Greece) 189 6282

Fantasia and Fugue in G minor, arranged by Mitropoulos

Minneapolis 6 April 1942	Minneapolis SO	78: Columbia (USA) X 244 LP: Ovation VM 5645 CD: Nickson NN 1002 CD: Discantus (Greece) 189 6212

Toccata, Adagio and Fugue in C, arranged by Weiner

Minneapolis 3-4 December 1940	Minneapolis SO	78: Columbia (USA) X 195 CD: Nickson NN 1002 CD: Discantus (Greece) 189 6212 Discantus incorrectly dated 1942

Wir glauben all' an einen Gott, arranged by Bösenroth

Minneapolis 6 April 1942	Minneapolis SO	78: Columbia (USA) X 244 CD: Nickson NN 1002 CD: Discantus (Greece) 189 6212
New York 23 December 1945	NBC SO	Unpublished radio broadcast

SAMUEL BARBER (1910-1981)

Vanessa

New York 1 February 1958	Metropolitan Opera Orchestra & Chorus Steber, Elias, Resnik, Gedda, Nagy, Tozzi Cehanovsky	Unpublished Met broadcast
New York 23 February- 10 April 1958	Metropolitan Opera Orchestra & Chorus Steber, Elias, Resnik, Gedda, Nagy, Tozzi, Cehanovsky	LP: Victor LM 6138/LSC 6138 CD: RCA/BMG RG 78992/GD 87899 Excerpts LP: Victor LM 6062/LSC 6062/ARL2-2094/ RL 020094/SP 33-21/RL 85177 CD: RCA/BMG 09026 615802

Medea's meditation and dance of vengeance

New York 16 March 1958	NYPSO	CD: As-Disc AS 543

BELA BARTOK (1881-1945)

Violin Rhapsody No 2

New York 7 November 1946	NYPSO Stern	Unpublished radio broadcast

ARNOLD BAX (1883-1953)

Overture to a Picaresque comedy

New York 22 April 1951	NYPSO	LP: Off-the-Air Record Club OTA 8

LUDWIG VAN BEETHOVEN (1770-1827)

Symphony No 1

New York 25 November 1951	NYPSO	LP: Melodram MEL 233 CD: Melodram MEL 18030 Incorrectly dated 1954
New York 31 January 1954	NYPSO	CD: As-Disc AS 517 CD: Notes PGP 11030 CD: Musica viva 196 0002

Symphony No 2

New York 22 January 1950	NYPSO	CD: Discantus (Greece) 189 6022
New York 29 November 1953	NYPSO	Unpublished radio broadcast

Symphony No 3 "Eroica"

Athens 2 October 1955	NYPSO	CD: Hellas (Greece) YPPO 1

Symphony No 5

New York 21 October 1956	NYPSO	LP: Musica viva 90031 CD: Musica viva 196 0002

Symphony No 6 "Pastoral"

Minneapolis 22 January 1940	Minneapolis SO	78: Columbia (USA) M 401 78: Columbia (Canada) D 35 LP: Columbia (USA) RL 3009/HL 7120 CD: Grammofono AB 78509/AB 78646-78649 CD: Theorema TH 121.132 CD: Iron Needle IN 1331 CD: Discantus (Greece) 189 6012

Symphony No 8

New York 5 May 1957	NYPSO	LP: Musica viva 90031 CD: As-Disc AS 517 CD: Notes PGP 11030 CD: Documents LV 976 CD: Discantus (Greece) 189 6012

Symphony No 9 "Choral"

New York 15 April 1955	NYPSO Westminster Choir Yeend, Lipton, Lloyd, Harrell	Unpublished radio broadcast

Piano Concerto No 3

New York 23 February 1957	NYPSO J.Casadesus	LP: Columbia (USA) C 10954

Piano Concerto No 4

New York 22 August 1943	NYPSO Hofmann	Unpublished radio broadcast
New York 8 January 1950	NYPSO Serkin	Unpublished radio broadcast
New York 22 April 1951	NYPSO Rubinstein	LP: Off-the-Air Record Club OTA 8 CD: As-Disc AS 532 CD: NotaBlu 935 10512 CD: Legends LGD 102 CD: Documents LV 980 CD: Discantus (Greece) 189 6032

Piano Concerto No 5 "Emperor"

Paris 19 September 1955	NYPSO R.Casadesus	LP: Columbia (USA) ML 5100/P 14201 LP: Philips ABL 3142/A01215L/ GBL 5613 LP: CBS 72312
Lucerne 1 September 1957	VPO R.Casadesus	Unpublished radio broadcast First movement CD: Relief (Switzerland) CR 1882

Violin Concerto

New York 15 January 1950	NYPSO Goldberg	LP: Melodram MEL 210
New York 26 October 1952	NYPSO Francescatti	CD: Melodram MEL 18030 Incorrectly dated 1956
New York 12 February 1956	NYPSO Heifetz	LP: Melodram MEL 210 LP: Movimento musica 01.005 LP: Arioso 15.001 CD: Prelude PRE 2160 CD: Sterling SOCD 1005

Coriolan, overture

Minneapolis 10 January 1940	Minneapolis SO	78: Columbia (USA) 11175D 78: Columbia LX 914 LP: Columbia (USA) RL 3038 CD: Nickson NN 1007 CD: Grammofono AB 78608/AB 78646-78649 CD: Discantus (Greece) 189 6032

Die Geschöpfe des Prometheus, excerpts

New York 21 February 1954	NYPSO	CD: As-Disc AS 532 CD: Legends LGD 102 CD: NotaBlu 935 106 CD: Discantus (Greece) 189 6032

Grosse Fuge

New York 2 January 1960	NYPSO	Unpublished radio broadcast

Leonore No 3, overture

Minneapolis 10 January 1940	Minneapolis SO	78: Columbia (USA) X 173 78: Columbia (Canada) J 34 LP: Columbia (USA) RL 3038 CD: Nickson NN 1006 CD: Grammofono AB 78608/AB 78646-78649 CD: Sony SX2K 62587/ASK 5633

Missa Solemnis

New York 8 November 1953	NYPSO Westminster Choir Steber, Tangeman, Smith-Spencer, Harrell	LP: Melodram MEL 233

ALBAN BERG (1885-1935)

Wozzeck

New York 12-15 April 1951	NYPSO Schola cantorum Farrell, Eustis, Mordino, D.Lloyd, Jagel, Harrell, Herbert, Anderson, Norville	LP: Columbia (USA) SL 118/Y2 33126 LP: Columbia (France) FCX 157-158 LP: Philips A01490-01491L/ ABL 3388-3389 LP: CBS M2P 42470 CD: Palladio PD 4126-4127 CD: Andromeda ANR 2514-2515 CD: Sony CD 42470/MH2K 62759 CD 42470 was announced but not issued Excerpts LP: Columbia (USA) BIM 13

Violin Concerto

New York 30 December 1945	NBC SO Szigeti	LP: Discocorp WSA 701 LP: Cetra DOC 3 LP: Melodiya D 029257 CD: Intaglio INCD 7061 CD: As-Disc AS 626 CD: Music and Arts CD 668 CD: Seven Seas (Japan) KICC 2209 CD: Dante LYS 067

ARTHUR BERGER (Born 1912)

Ideas of order

New York 12 April 1953	NYPSO	Unpublished radio broadcast World premiere performance

HECTOR BERLIOZ (1803-1869)

Symphonie fantastique

New York 24 February 1957	NYPSO	LP: Columbia (USA) ML 5188/MS 6030/ 3216 0204/ST 164 LP: Philips A01354L/SABL 108 LP: CBS 61465/73144/78211 LP: Melodiya C 1014079 CD: Sony MPK 45685 Excerpt LP: Columbia (USA) 6P-6209
Rochester NY 14 April 1957	NYPSO	CD: Hunt CD 562 CD: Discantus 189 6332 CD: Music and Arts CD 562

Roméo et Juliette, orchestral suite

New York 27 October 1952	NYPSO	LP: Columbia (USA) ML 4632/P 14177 LP: Philips NBL 5028 CD: Sony SX2K 62587 Excerpt CD: Sony SSK 6368/MXK 6281

Grande messe des morts

Salzburg 15 August 1956	VPO Vienna Opera Chorus Simoneau	LP: Cetra LO 59 LP: Movimento musica 02.024 CD: Orfeo C457 971B LP editions include spoken introduction by Mitropoulos, in which he dedicates the performance to the memory of Wilhelm Furtwängler
Cologne 26 August 1956	WDR Orchestra and Chorus Gedda	CD: Hunt CD 562 CD: Discantus (Greece) 189 6332 CD: Tahra TAH 209-211 Hunt and Tahra dated 1957

Les nuits d'été

Atlanta 5 April 1953	NYPSO Steber	CD: As-Disc AS 619
New York 21 January 1954	Columbia SO Steber	LP: Columbia (USA) ML 4940/ML 5843/ Y 32360 LP: Philips NBL 5029 LP: CBS 61430 CD: Sony MHK 62356

Benvenuto Cellini, overture

New York 26 April 1953	NYPSO	CD: As-Disc AS 619 Incorrectly dated 1956

Rob Roy, overture

New York 1 April 1951	NYPSO	CD: As-Disc AS 619

Le roi Lear, overture

New York 30 December 1945	NBC SO	CD: As-Disc AS 619 CD: Discantus (Greece) 189 6332

GEORGES BIZET (1838-1875)

Carmen

New York 12 January 1957	Metropolitan Opera Orchestra & Chorus Stevens, Amara, Del Monaco, Guarrera	LP: Hope Records HOPE 210 LP: Cetra LO 48/DOC 45 LP: Paragon DSV 52002 CD: Nuova era NE 2307-2308 CD: Discantus (Greece) 189 6292 Excerpts LP: Di Stefano GDS 4001 LP: Melodram MEL 675 CD: Discantus (Greece) 189 6292

Symphony in C

New York 25 April 1954	NYPSO	CD: As-Disc AS 617

ARTHUR BLISS (1891-1975)

Piano Concerto

New York 9 January 1960	NYPSO Bachauer	Unpublished radio broadcast

ΠΡΟΓΡΑΜΜΑ

ΜΕΡΟΣ ΠΡΩΤΟΝ

1) ***Φιδέλιο*** (εἰσαγωγὴ) . . . . L. van BEETHOVEN
ὑπὸ τῆς ὀρχήστρας

2) ***Κοντσέρτο*** διὰ βιολὶ . . . . L. van BEETHOVEN
I Allegro ma non troppo
II Larghetto
III Rondo
Ὁ κ. *B. Huberman* καὶ ἡ ὀρχήστρα.

ΜΕΡΟΣ ΔΕΥΤΕΡΟΝ

3) ***Ἀκαδημαϊκὴ εἰσαγωγὴ*** . . . . . . J. BRAHMS
ὑπὸ τῆς ὀρχήστρας

4) ***Κοντσέρτο*** διὰ βιολὶ . . . . J. BRAHMS
I Allegro non troppo
II Adagio
III Allegro giocoso, ma non troppo vivace.
Ὁ κ. *Br. Huberman* καὶ ἡ ὀρχήστρα.

ΑΙΘΟΥΣΑ ΩΔΕΙΟΥ ΑΘΗΝΩΝ

1871

ΣΥΜΦΩΝΙΚΑΙ ΚΑΙ ΛΑΪΚΑΙ ΣΥΝΑΥΛΙΑΙ

ΑΙΘΟΥΣΑ "ΑΤΤΙΚΟΥ"

Κυριακὴ 4 Μαρτίου 1928, ὥρα 10 3/4 π.μ. ἀκριβῶς

ΣΥΝΑΥΛΙΑ

ΠΕΜΠΤΗ ΣΥΝΔΡΟΜΗΤΩΝ

ΤΗΣ

ΣΥΜΦΩΝΙΚΗΣ ΟΡΧΗΣΤΡΑΣ

ΤΟΥ

ΩΔΕΙΟΥ ΑΘΗΝΩΝ

ΠΕΡΙΟΔΟΣ 1927 — 1928

ΔΙΕΥΘΥΝΤΗΣ ΟΡΧΗΣΤΡΑΣ

Δ. ΜΗΤΡΟΠΟΥΛΟΣ

ΣΟΛΙΣΤ

Ο ΠΑΓΚΟΣΜΙΟΥ ΦΗΜΗΣ ΚΑΛΛΙΤΕΧΝΗΣ

BRON. HUBERMAN

(βιολὶ)

Μετὰ τὴν ἔναρξιν τῆς Συναυλίας ἡ εἴσοδος ἐπιτρέπεται μόνον κατὰ τὰ διαλείμματα.

ΤΥΠΟΙΣ ΕΤΑΙΡΕΙΑΣ -Π. Δ. ΣΑΚΕΛΛΑΡΙΟΣ - 4053

Τιμὴ ἀναλυτικοῦ προγράμματος Δρ. 5.

ERNEST BLOCH (1880-1959)

Schelomo for cello and orchestra

New York 8 April 1951	NYPSO Rose	Unpublished radio broadcast
New York 21 April 1951	NYPSO Rose	LP: Columbia (USA) ML 4425/P 14167
New York 19 February 1956	NYPSO L.Varga	Unpublished radio broadcast

ALEXANDER BORODIN (1833-1887)

Symphony No 2

Minneapolis 7 December 1941	Minneapolis SO	78: Columbia (USA) M 528 CD: Nickson NN 1003 CD: Discantus (Greece) 189 6222
New York 2 November 1953	NYPSO	LP: Columbia (USA) ML 4966/P 14195 LP: Philips ABL 3079/A01227L CD: Grammofono AB 78509/AB 78646-78648 CD: Iron Needle Grammofono and Iron Needle incorrectly describe this as Minneapolis 1941

In the Steppes of Central Asia

New York 20 March 1953	NYPSO	45: Philips N02107L LP: Columbia (USA) ML 4815/CL 751 LP: Philips A01227L/NBL 5015/
New York 19 April 1953	NYPSO	CD: As-Disc AS 508 CD: Legends LGD 107 CD: Discantus (Greece) 189 6222

Polovtsian Dances

New York 1 December 1952	NYPSO	45: Columbia (USA) A 1823 45: Philips ABE 10011/N02107L LP: Columbia (USA) ML 4815/CL 751 LP: Philips A01160L/A01227L/ NBL 5015 CD: Sony (Greece) awaiting publication

JOHANNES BRAHMS (1833-1897)

Symphony No 2

New York 20 August 1944	NYPSO	Unpublished radio broadcast

Symphony No 3

New York 20 April 1952	NYPSO	CD: As-Disc AS 625 CD: Notes PGP 11008 CD: Discantus (Greece) 189 6042
Florence 17 June 1953	Maggio musicale Orchestra	LP: Cetra DOC 64
New York 9 February 1958	NYPSO	LP: Cetra DOC 23 CD: Hunt CDLSMH 34020/CDMP 420 Third movement CD: Melodram MEL 18009 CD: Discantus (Greece) 189 6062
Salzburg 10 August 1958	Concertgebouw Orchestra	CD: Orfeo C458 797B

Symphony No 4

New York 1 January 1950	NYPSO	Unpublished radio broadcast
New York 22 November 1953	NYPSO	CD: As-Disc AS 625 CD: Notes PGP 11008 CD: Discantus (Greece) 189 6042
New York 28 October 1956	NYPSO	LP: Cetra DOC 24 CD: Hunt CDLSMH 34020/CDMP 420

Piano Concerto No 1

New York 12 April 1953	NYPSO Kapell	CD: Hunt CD 736 CD: Melodram MEL 18009 CD: Music and Arts CD 990 CD: Discantus (Greece) 189 6062
New York 13 February 1955	NYPSO	CD: As-Disc AS 610 CD: NotaBlu 935 10634

Piano Concerto No 2

New York 6 April 1952	NYPSO R.Casadesus	CD: Discantus (Greece) 189 6072

Violin Concerto

New York 24 October 1948	NYPSO Szigeti	CD: As-Disc AS 518 CD: Legend LGD 135 CD: Discantus (Greece) 189 6052
Salzburg 24 August 1958	VPO Francescatti	CD: Intaglio INCD 7061 Grandi concerti LP GCL 12 purporting to contain this performance actually has Francescatti's commercial recording conducted by Bernstein, with audience noise added to simulate a live version

Double Concerto

New York 20 August 1944	NYPSO Corigliano, Rose	Unpublished radio broadcast

Academic Festival Overture

New York 9 February 1958	NYPSO	LP: Cetra DOC 23 LP: New York Philharmonic NYP 87 CD: Hunt CD 736 CD: Melodram MEL 18009 CD: Discantus (Greece) 189 6061 Discantus incorrectly dated 1953

Haydn Variations

Minneapolis 4 April 1942	Minneapolis SO	78: Columbia (USA) X 225 LP: Columbia (USA) RL 3038 CD: Nickson NN 1007 CD: Discantus (Greece) 189 6072
New York 13 February 1955	NYPSO	LP: New York Philharmonic NYP 87
Seattle 8 May 1955	NYPSO	CD: As-Disc AS 610 CD: Hunt CD 736/CDGI 736 CD: NotaBlu 935 10634 CD: Discantus (Greece) 189 6052
Athens 2 October 1955	NYPSO	CD: Hellas (Greece) YPPO 2

MAX BRUCH (1838-1920)

Violin Concerto No 1

New York 4 January 1952	NYPSO Francescatti	LP: Columbia (USA) ML 4575 LP: Philips A01610R/ABR 4011 CD: Sony MH2K 62339 Excerpt LP: Philips GBL 5534

FERRUCCIO BUSONI (1866-1924)

Arlecchino

New York 14 October 1951	NYPSO Polisi, Lipton, D.Lloyd, Pease, Wildermann, Brownlee, Alden-Edkins Sung in English	LP: Off-the-Air Record Club OTA 12

Indian Fantasy for piano and orchestra

New York 28 December 1941	NYPSO Petri	Unpublished radio broadcast Issued on cassette only

Violin Concerto

New York 28 December 1941	NYPSO Szigeti	Unpublished radio broadcast

2 Studies for Doktor Faust

New York 28 December 1941	NYPSO	Unpublished radio broadcast

MINNEAPOLIS SYMPHONY ORCHESTRA

Thirty-fifth Season, 1937–1938

DIMITRI MITROPOULOS
Conductor

DANIELE AMFITHEATROF
Associate Conductor

Eighth Evening Concert

FRIDAY EVENING, JANUARY 21, 1938, AT 8:30

MITROPOULOS

Conductor-Pianist

PROGRAM

1 Symphony No. 3 ("Eroica"), in E-flat major, Op. 55 - - - - - - - - - - *Beethoven*

I. Allegro con brio
II. Marcia funebre: Adagio assai
III. Scherzo: Allegro vivace
IV. Finale: Allegro molto

INTERMISSION

2 Fantaisie for Piano and Orchestra - - - *Louis Aubert*

Dimitri Mitropoulos playing the piano part
(First time in Minneapolis)

3 Adagio for Strings, Op. 3 - - - - - - - *Lekeu*

4 "La Valse," a Choreographic Poem - - - - *Ravel*

The Steinway is the Official Piano of the Minneapolis Symphony Orchestra
Victor Records

Next Sunday Concert, January 23, at 3:15 P. M.
Next Friday Concert, January 28, at 8:30 P. M.

MINNEAPOLIS SYMPHONY ORCHESTRA

Thirty-fifth Season, 1937–1938

DIMITRI MITROPOULOS
Conductor

DANIELE AMFITHEATROF
Associate Conductor

Ninth Evening Concert

FRIDAY EVENING, JANUARY 28, 1938, AT 8:30

MITROPOULOS, *Conductor*

Soloist: ARTUR RUBINSTEIN, *Pianist*

PROGRAM

1 Symphony No. 1, in D major - - - - - - *Mahler*

I. Langsam—Schleppend wie ein Naturlaut
(Slow—Spun out as a sound of Nature)
II. Kräftig bewegt (Strongly agitated)
III. Feierlich und gemessen (In a solemn and measured manner)
IV. Stürmisch bewegt (Stormily)

(First time in Minneapolis)

INTERMISSION

2 Concerto for Piano and Orchestra, No. 4, in G major, Op. 58 - - - - - - - - - - *Beethoven*

I. Allegro moderato
II. Andante con moto
III. Rondo: Vivace

(The Rondo follows the Andante without pause)

Mr. Rubinstein uses the Steinway Piano

The Steinway is the Official Piano of the Minneapolis Symphony Orchestra
Victor Records

Next Concert, Sunday, January 30, at 5:15 P. M.
Next Symphony Concert, THURSDAY, February 3, at 8:30 P. M.

EMMANUEL CHABRIER (1841-1894)

Marche joyeuse

Minneapolis 7 December 1941	Minneapolis SO	78: Columbia (USA) 19013D 45: Columbia (USA) 3-201 LP: Nickson NH 1001 CD: Nickson NN 1004 CD: Dante LYS 211 CD: Discantus (Greece) 189 6272
New York 16 April 1950	NYPSO	Unpublished radio broadcast

YVES CHARDON (Born 1902)

Rhumba for cello and orchestra

Minneapolis 2 March 1945	Minneapolis SO Chardon	78: Columbia (USA) 13104D CD: Nickson NN 1002 CD: Dante LYS 211

ERNEST CHAUSSON (1855-1899)

Symphony in B flat

Minneapolis 9 March 1946	Minneapolis SO	78: Columbia (USA) MM 825 LP: Columbia (USA) ML 4141/P 14149 CD: Nickson NN 1008-1009
New York 26 April 1953	NYPSO	CD: As-Disc AS 617 CD: Discantus (Greece) 189 6272

Poème pour violon et orchestre

New York 29 December 1940	NYPSO Spalding	Unpublished radio broadcast

FREDERIC CHOPIN (1810-1849)

Piano Concerto No 1

Minneapolis 6 December 1941	Minneapolis SO Kilenyi	78: Columbia (USA) M 515 LP: Columbia (USA) RL 3028 CD: Nickson NN 1008-1009 CD: Discantus (Greece) 189 6302

Chopiniana, suite arranged by Rogal-Lewitzsky

Philadelphia 21 September 1945	Philadelphia Orchestra	78: Columbia (USA) M 598 78: Columbia (Canada) D 139 78: Columbia (Brazil) 30-5401-5403 CD: Nickson NN 1008-1009 CD: Grammofono AB 78646-78649 CD: Iron Needle IN 1327 CD: Discantus (Greece) 189 6302 Orchestra described for this recording as Robin Hood Dell Orchestra; Grammofono incorrectly describes orchestra as Minneapolis SO

DOMENICO CIMAROSA (1749-1801)

La bella Grecia, overture

New York 21 February 1954	NYPSO	CD: As-Disc AS 539 CD: NotaBlu 935 10512 CD: Discantus (Greece) 189 6192

AARON COPLAND (1900-1990)

Appalachian Spring

New York 7 February 1954	NYPSO	CD: As-Disc AS 543

FRANCOIS COUPERIN (1668-1733)

La sultane, Overture and Allegro arranged by Milhaud

Minneapolis 2 March 1945	Minneapolis SO	78: Columbia (USA) 12161D CD: Nickson NN 1002 CD: Discantus (Greece) 189 6282
New York 30 December 1945	NBC SO	Unpublished radio broadcast
New York 4 January 1952	NYPSO	LP: Columbia (USA) AAL 16

CLAUDE DEBUSSY (1862-1918)

La mer

New York 27 November 1950	NYPSO	LP: Columbia (USA) ML 4344/P 14168 LP: Philips A01100L/A06683R
Cologne 24 October 1960	WDR Orchestra	CD: Hunt CDGI 753 CD: Discantus (Greece) 189 6232

Ibéria (Images pour orchestre)

New York 7 February 1954	NYPSO	CD: As-Disc AS 617 CD: Discantus (Greece) 189 6232

VINCENT D'INDY (1851-1931)

Wallenstein, 3 symphonic overtures after Schiller

New York 28 October 1951	NYPSO	Unpublished radio broadcast

PAUL DUKAS (1865-1935)

L'apprenti sorcier

Minneapolis 3 December 1940	Minneapolis SO	78: Columbia (USA) X 212 78: Columbia LX 25006-25007 LP: Columbia (USA) RL 3021/HL 7129 CD: Nickson NN 1004 CD: Grammofono AB 78646-78649 CD: Dante LYS 211 CD: Discantus (Greece) 189 6232
New York 2 November 1956	NYPSO	45: Philips A409 094E LP: Columbia (USA) ML 5198 CD: Sony ASK 5633/SX2K 62587

ANTONIN DVORAK (1841-1904)

Cello Concerto

Minneapolis 4 April 1942	Minneapolis SO Piatigorsky	Columbia unpublished

Violin Concerto

New York 4 March 1951	NYPSO Stern	LP: Movimento musica 01.068 CD: Movimento musica 011.006 CD: Bella musica 31.6009 Bella musica incorrectly states that recording made in Berlin

Slavonic Dance No 1 in C

Minneapolis 3 December 1940	Minneapolis SO	78: Columbia (USA) 11645D LP: Columbia (USA) HL 7129 CD: Nickson NN 1004 CD: Discantus (Greece) 189 6202

Slavonic Dance No 3 in A flat

Minneapolis 3 December 1940	Minneapolis SO	78: Columbia (USA) 11645D LP: Columbia (USA) HL 7129 LP: Ovation VM 5645 CD: Nickson NN 1004 CD: Discantus (Greece) 189 6202

GOTTFRIED VON EINEM (1918-1996)

Capriccio for orchestra

New York 18 October 1953	NYPSO	Unpublished radio broadcast

MANUEL DE FALLA (1876-1946)

El sombrero de 3 picos, dances

New York 2 November 1953	NYPSO	45: Philips ABE 10005/A400 010E LP: Columbia (USA) ML 5172/AL 44/BLD 7098

La vida breve, Interlude and Dance

New York 2 November 1953	NYPSO	LP: Columbia (USA) ML 5172/AL 44/BLD 7098 LP: Philips L00453L

Noches en los jardines de Espana

New York 2 November 1956- 21 March 1957	NYPSO R.Casadesus	LP: Columbia (USA) ML 5172/BLD 7098 LP: Philips L01361L

Homenajes para orquesta

New York 10-11 April 1954	NYPSO	Unpublished radio broadcast

LUKAS FOSS (Born 1922)

Psalms for chorus and orchestra

New York 12 May 1957	NYPSO Schola cantorum	Unpublished radio broadcast

CESAR FRANCK (1822-1890)

Symphony in D minor

Minneapolis 8 January- 26 November 1940	Minneapolis SO	78: Columbia (USA) M 436 78: Columbia (Argentina) 266155-266159 LP: Columbia (USA) RL 3006/HL 7102 CD: Nickson NN 1005 CD: Discantus (Greece) 189 6272

Variations symphoniques pour piano et orchestre

New York 19 April 1953	NYPSO Rubinstein	CD: As-Disc AS 508 CD: Music and Arts CD 655 CD: Documents LV 980 CD: Legends LGD 107

Prélude, chorale et fugue, arranged by Pierné

New York 28 October 1951	NYPSO	Unpublished radio broadcast

ALBERTO GINASTERA (1916-1983)

Creole Faust, overture

New York 24 February 1957	NYPSO	CD: As-Disc AS 543

ALEXANDER GLAZUNOV (1865-1936)

Violin Concerto

New York 2 May 1954	NYPSO Rabin	Unpublished radio broadcast

Overture on Greek themes

Minneapolis 6 April 1942	Minneapolis SO	78: Columbia (USA) X 228 78: Columbia (Australia) LOX 552-553 LP: Nickson NH 1001 CD: Nickson NN 1002

REINHOLD GLIERE (1875-1956)

Sailors' dance (The Red Poppy)

Minneapolis 7 December 1941	Minneapolis SO	78: Columbia (USA) M 528/12899D LP: Columbia (USA) RL 3021/HL 7129 CD: Nickson NN 1004

MIKHAIL GLINKA (1804-1857)

Russlan and Ludmila, overture

New York 26 February 1956	NYPSO	CD: As-Disc AS 502

KARL GOLDMARK (1830-1915)

Violin Concerto No 1

New York 3 February 1957	NYPSO Milstein	CD: Discantus (Greece) 189 6202

MORTON GOULD (1913-1996)

Fall River Legend, ballet suite

New York 31 March 1952	NYPSO	LP: Columbia (USA) ML 4616 LP: New World Records NW 253

Philharmonic Waltzes

New York 23 January 1950	NYPSO	78: Columbia (USA) 13139D LP: Columbia (USA) ML 2167/BM 39

Minstrel Show

Minneapolis 20 January 1947	Minneapolis SO	78: Victor 11-9654 LP: Nickson NH 1001 CD: Nickson NN 1005

Jekyll and Hyde variations

New York 3 February 1957	NYPSO	Unpublished radio broadcast

EDVARD GRIEG (1843-1907)

2 Elegiac melodies

Minneapolis 3 December 1940	Minneapolis SO	78: Columbia (USA) 11698D 78: Columbia (Argentina) 266089 CD: Nickson NN 1002

CAMARGO GUARNIERI (1907-1993)

Prologo y fuga

New York 16 March 1958	NYPSO	CD: As-Disc AS 543

GEORGE FRIDERIC HANDEL (1685-1759)

Largo, arranged by Molinari

Minneapolis 6 April 1942	Minneapolis SO	Columbia unpublished

FRANZ JOSEF HAYDN (1732-1809)

Symphony No 80

New York 7 February 1954	NYPSO	CD: As-Disc AS 539 CD: Discantus (Greece) 189 6192

Symphony No 100 "Military"

New York 4 November 1956	NYPSO	CD: As-Disc AS 539 CD: NotaBlu 935.10512 CD: Documents LV 976 CD: Discantus (Greece) 189 6192

Overture in D (Overture to an English opera)

New York 7 February 1954	NYPSO	CD: As-Disc AS 539 CD: Discantus (Greece) 189 6192

PAUL HINDEMITH (1895-1963)

Die Harmonie der Welt

New York 25 October 1953	NYPSO	CD: As-Disc AS 540

Sonata for oboe and piano

New York 21 April 1952	Gomberg Mitropoulos, piano	LP: Columbia (USA) ML 5603

MIKHAIL IPPOLITOV-IVANOV (1859-1935)

Caucasian Sketches

New York 20 March 1953	NYPSO	45: Columbia (USA) A 1824 LP: Columbia (USA) ML 4815/CL 751 LP: Philips NBL 5015/N02107L/S06626L

DMITRI KABALEVSKY (1904-1987)

Symphony No 4

New York 3 November 1957	NYPSO	Unpublished radio broadcast US premiere performance

Colas Breugnon, overture

New York 3 November 1957	NYPSO	Unpublished private recording

FRANCIS SCOTT KEY (1779-1843)

The Star-spangled Banner, march

New York 11 November 1957	NYPSO	Columbia unpublished

ARAM KHACHATURIAN (1903-1978)

Piano Concerto

New York 3 January 1950	NYPSO Levant	78: Columbia (USA) MM 905 LP: Columbia (USA) ML 4288/P 14162 LP: Columbia (France) FCX 136

LEON KIRCHNER (Born 1919)

Piano Concerto

New York 24 February 1956	NYPSO Kirchner	LP: Columbia (USA) ML 5185/CML 5185 LP: New World Records NW 286

ZOLTAN KODALY (1882-1967)

Dances from Galanta

New York 25 January 1954	NYPSO	Columbia unpublished

Hary Janos, suite

New York 27 February 1956	NYPSO	LP: Columbia (USA) ML 5101/P 14202

Psalmus hungaricus

New York 12 May 1957	NYPSO Schola cantorum D.Lloyd	Unpublished radio broadcast

ERNST KRENEK (1900-1991)

Ballad of the railroads

New York 5 April 1950	Steber Mitropoulos, piano	Unpublished radio broadcast

Cantata for wartime

Minneapolis 24 March 1944	Minneapolis SO University Choir Peterson	Unpublished radio broadcast

Piano Concerto

New York 11 December 1949	NYPSO Mitropoulos, piano	CD: As-Disc AS 512

Symphonic elegy in memoriam Anton von Webern

New York 21 April 1951	NYPSO	LP: Columbia (USA) ML 4524 LP: Philips ABL 3393 CD: Sony MH2K 62759

Symphonic movements on a North Carolina folktune

Boston 23 December 1944	Boston SO	Unpublished radio broadcast

PAUL LADMIRAULT (1877-1944)

Variations sur des airs de Biniou

New York 3 April 1955	NYPSO	Unpublished radio broadcast

EDOUARD LALO (1823-1892)

Symphonie espagnole pour violon et orchestre

New York 4 November 1956	NYPSO Hagen	Unpublished radio broadcast
New York 22 April 1957	NYPSO Francescatti	LP: Columbia (USA) ML 5184/ML 5601/ MS 6201/MP 38761/Y 33229 LP: Philips ABL 3296/L01361L LP: CBS 60262/72321 CD: Sony MH2K 62339 <u>Excerpts</u> LP: Columbia (USA) ML 5693/MS 6293/ PM 1/PMS 1

Le roi d'Ys, overture

Minneapolis 2 March 1945	Minneapolis SO	78: Columbia (USA) MX 343 LP: Columbia (USA) ML 2123/HL 7129 CD: Nickson NN 1008-1009 CD: Dante LYS 211 CD: Discantus (Greece) 189 6292
New York 25 April 1954	NYPSO	Unpublished radio broadcast

RUGGERO LEONCAVALLO (1857-1919)

I pagliacci

New York 3 January 1959	Metropolitan Opera Orchestra & Chorus Amara, Del Monaco, Anthony, Warren, Sereni	CD: Melodram CDM 27013 CD: Hunt CDMP 473 CD: Discantus (Greece) 189 6252 <u>Excerpts</u> LP: Gioielli della lirica GML 11 LP: Foyer FO 1035 LP: Joker SM 1299/SM 1353
New York 30 January 1960	Metropolitan Opera Orchestra & Chorus Amara, Baum, Anthony, Merrill, Guarrera	Unpublished Met broadcast

FRANZ LISZT (1811-1886)

Piano Concerto No 1

Florence 17 June 1953	Maggio musicale Orchestra Michelangeli	LP: Cetra DOC 64

Rapsodie espagnole for piano and orchestra, arranged by Busoni

Minneapolis 10 January 1940	Minneapolis SO Petri	78: Columbia (USA) X 163 78: Columbia LX 891-892 78: Columbia (Canada) CJ 8 78: Columbia (Australia) LOX 562-563 78: Columbia (Argentina) 264700-264701 78: Columbia (Brazil) 30/5227-5228 LP: Columbia (USA) RL 3040 CD: Pearl GEMMCD 9347 CD: Nickson NN 1003 CD: Appian APR 7023 CD: Discantus (Greece) 189 6302

Les Préludes

New York 24 February 1956	NYPSO	Columbia unpublished
New York 27 February 1956	NYPSO	LP: Columbia (USA) ML 5198 CD: Palladio PD 4104 CD: Theorema TH 121.146 CD: Legends LGD 147

CHARLES LOEFFLER (1861-1935)

2 Rhapsodies for oboe, viola and piano

New York 21 April 1952	Gomberg, Katims, Mitropoulos, piano	LP: Columbia (USA) ML 5603 CD: Pantheon Legends

JEAN-BAPTISTE LULLY (1632-1687)

Menuet (Le temple de la paix), arranged by Mottl

Minneapolis 3 December 1940	Minneapolis SO	78: Columbia (USA) X 197/12900D 78: Columbia (Canada) 15462 78: Columbia (Argentina) 266199 LP: Nickson NH 1001 CD: Nickson NN 1004

GUSTAV MAHLER (1860-1911)

Symphony No 1

Minneapolis 4 November 1940	Minneapolis SO	78: Columbia (USA) M 469 78: Columbia (Australia) LOX 530-535 LP: Columbia (USA) ML 4251/RL 3120/ P 14157 LP: Columbia 33CX 1068 CD: Grammofono AB 78566/AB 78646-78649 CD: Theorema TH 121.152 CD: Biddulph WHL 031-032 CD: Sirio SO 5300.30 CD: Sony MHK 62342 First recording of the symphony
New York 21 October 1951	NYPSO	LP: Cetra LO 514 LP: Musica viva 90032 CD: Hunt CDHP 593
New York 9 January 1960	NYPSO	LP: Cetra DOC 43 CD: Hunt CD 556/CDHP 556 CD: Musica viva 88005 CD: Discantus (Greece) 189 6082

A version of the symphony on Grandi concerti LP GCL 20 attributed to Mitropoulos and dated June 1955 is identical to the edition conducted by Bruno Walter on the Movimento musica label: Mitropoulos did not conduct the work in 1955

Symphony No 3

New York 15 April 1956	NYPSO Westminster Choir B.Krebs	LP: Cetra LO 514/DOC 43 CD: Hunt CD 557 CD: Documents LV 1000-1001
Cologne 31 October 1960	WDR Orchestra and Chorus West	LP: Rococo 2055 LP: Cetra DOC 4 LP: Movimento musica 02.016 CD: Hunt CDHP 593 CD: Discantus (Greece) 189 6092 CD: Tahra TAH 209-211

Symphony No 5

New York 21 January 1960	NYPSO	LP: Replica ARPL 32463 LP: Cetra DOC 43 LP: New York Philharmonic NYP 88 LP: Movimento musica 02.005 LP: Musica viva 90033 CD: Hunt CD 523/CDHP 523 CD: Musica viva 88054 CD: Discantus (Greece) 189 6132 Movimento musica incorrectly dated 1955

Symphony No 6

New York 10 April 1955	NYPSO	LP: Replica ARPL 32463 LP: Cetra DOC 43
Cologne 31 August 1959	WDR Orchestra	LP: Cetra DOC 5 LP: Movimento musica 02.015 CD: Hunt CD 522/CDHP 522 CD: Discantus (Greece) 189 6112

Symphony No 8 "Symphony of a thousand"

Salzburg 28 August 1960	VPO Wiener Singverein Vienna Opera Chorus Vienna Boys' Choir Coertse, Zadek, West, Malaniuk, Zampieri, Prey, Edelmann	LP: Everest SDBR 3189/SDBR 3441 LP: Ars nova C25-125 LP: Sine qua non SQN 18 CD: Hunt CD 558/CDHP 558 CD: Documents LV 1000-1001 CD: Discantus (Greece) 189 6122 Some editions incorrectly describe orchestra as Vienna Festival Orchestra

Symphony No 9

Vienna 28 September 1959	Concertgebouw Orchestra	Unpublished radio broadcast
New York 23 January 1960	NYPSO	LP: Replica RPL 2460-2461 LP: Cetra DOC 43 LP: Movimento musica 02.026 CD: Hunt CD 521/CDHP 521 CD: Discantus (Greece) 189 6142

Adagio (Symphony No 10)

New York 17 January 1960	NYPSO	LP: Replica RPL 2460-2461 LP: Cetra DOC 43 LP: Movimento musica 02.005 CD: Hunt CD 556/CDHP 556 CD: Musica viva 88005 CD: Discantus (Greece) 189 6082 Movimento musica incorrectly dated 1955

GIAN FRANCESCO MALIPIERO (1882-1973)

Symphony No 7 "Delle canzoni"

Turin May 1950	RAI Torino Orchestra	LP: Cetra LPC 50044

FRANK MARTIN (1890-1974)

Violin Concerto

New York 16 November 1952	NYPSO Szigeti	CD: As-Disc AS 620 CD: Music and Arts CD 720 CD: Seven Seas (Japan) KICC 2208

PIETRO MASCAGNI (1863-1945)

Cavalleria rusticana

New York 3 January 1959	Metropolitan Opera Orchestra & Chorus Milanov, Votipka, Elias, Barioni, Zanasi	CD: Hunt CDMP 472
New York 30 January 1960	Metropolitan Opera Orchestra & Chorus Rankin, Votipka, Vanni, Peerce, Cassel	Unpublished Met broadcast

Cavalleria rusticana, excerpt (Mamma, quel vino è generoso!)

Detroit 7 October 1945	Detroit SO Björling	V-Disc 623B CD: Nickson NN 1003 Orchestra described for this recording as Ford Symphony Orchestra

Cavalleria rusticana, intermezzo

Philadelphia 26 July 1946	Philadelphia Orchestra	78: Columbia (USA) X 317 45: Columbia (USA) AL 1637/A409 528E LP: Columbia (USA) ML 2053 Orchestra described for this recording as Robin Hood Dell Orchestra

JULES MASSENET (1842-1912)

Scènes alsaciennes

Minneapolis 11 March 1946	Minneapolis SO	78: Columbia (USA) MM 723 LP: Columbia (USA) ML 2074 CD: Dante LYS 211

Thaïs, Méditation

Minneapolis 6 April 1942	Minneapolis SO	Columbia unpublished

FELIX MENDELSSOHN-BARTHOLDY (1809-1847)

Symphony No 3 "Scotch"

Minneapolis 6 December 1941	Minneapolis SO	78: Columbia (USA) M 540 LP: Columbia (USA) RL 3017 CD: Nickson NN 1010 CD: Dante LYS 172
New York 2 November 1953	NYPSO	LP: Columbia (USA) ML 4864/P 14189 LP: Philips ABL 3082/A01174L/GBL 5550 CD: Theorema TH 121.135 Third movement LP: Columbia (USA) ML 5227
Salzburg 21 August 1960	BPO	CD: Tahra TAH 209-211
Cologne 24 October 1960	WDR Orchestra	LP: Grandi concerti GCL 33 CD: Virtuoso 269.7032 CD: Hunt CDGI 753 CD: Discantus (Greece) 189 6312

Symphony No 5 "Reformation"

New York 2 November 1953	NYPSO	LP: Columbia (USA) ML 4864/P 14189 LP: Philips ABL 3082/A01174L/GBL 5550 CD: Theorema 121.135 Third movement LP: Columbia (USA) ML 5227
Cologne 19 July 1957	WDR Orchestra	LP: Movimento musica 01.031 LP: Arioso 15006

Violin Concerto

New York 15 November 1953	NYPSO Elman	CD: As-Disc AS 629 CD: Seven Seas (Japan) KICC 2186 CD: Music and Arts CD 868 CD: Discantus (Greece) 189 6312
New York 17 November 1954	NYPSO Francescatti	LP: Columbia (USA) ML 4965/A 1109/72305 LP: Philips ABL 3159/A01214L CD: Sony MXK 62817/SSK 6368/MH2K 62339 Excerpts LP: Columbia (USA) D 2 LP: Philips GBL 5534

Capriccio brillant for piano and orchestra

Minneapolis 4 December 1940	Minneapolis SO J.Graudan	78: Columbia (USA) X 197 78: Columbia (Canada) J 59 78: Columbia (Argentina) 266198-266199 LP: Columbia (USA) ML 4127 CD: Nickson NN 1003 CD: Dante LYS 172

Scherzo (Octet for strings)

Minneapolis 10 January 1940	Minneapolis SO	78: Columbia (USA) X 166 78: Columbia LX 924 LP: Nickson NH 1001 CD: Dante LYS 172

Hebrides, overture

New York 11 March 1951	NYPSO	CD: As-Disc AS 620 CD: Discantus (Greece) 189 6312
New York 2 November 1953	NYPSO	45: Philips ABE 10006 LP: Columbia (USA) AL 52

Meeresstille glückliche Fahrt, overture

New York 2 November 1953	NYPSO	Columbia unpublished

Ruy Blas, overture

New York 2 November 1953	NYPSO	45: Philips ABE 10006/A409 012E LP: Columbia (USA) AL 52/A 1923

Elijah

New York 13 April 1952	NYPSO Westminster Choir Greer, Lipton, Tucker, Ligetti	Unpublished radio broadcast

PETER MENNIN (1923-1983)

Symphony No 3

New York 1 February 1954	NYPSO	LP: Columbia (USA) ML 4902 LP: Composers' Recordings SD 278 CD: Composers' Recordings CD 741

GIAN CARLO MENOTTI (Born 1911)

Sebastian, ballet suite

Philadelphia 26 July 1946	Philadelphia Orchestra	78: Columbia (USA) X 278 LP: Columbia (USA) ML 2053 Orchestra described for this recording as Robin Hood Dell Orchestra

GIACOMO MEYERBEER (1791-1864)

Coronation March (Le prophète)

Minneapolis 7 December 1941	Minneapolis SO	78: Columbia (USA) 19013D LP: Columbia (USA) HL 7129/3-201 CD: Nickson NN 1004 CD: Discantus (Greece) 189 6292 Discantus incorrectly dated 1945

DARIUS MILHAUD (1892-1974)

Christophe Colombe

New York 9 November 1952	NYPSO Dow, D.Lloyd, Harrell, Scott, Brownlee	Unpublished radio broadcast

Le boeuf sur le toit

Minneapolis 2 March 1945	Minneapolis SO	78: Columbia (USA) MX 308 LP: Columbia (USA) ML 2032 CD: Nickson NN 1004

CLAUDIO MONTEVERDI (1567-1643)

L'Orfeo, arranged by Respighi

New York 24 February 1952	NYPSO Schola cantorum Greer, Hobson, Kullmann, D.Lloyd, Harrell	Unpublished radio broadcast Complete performance may not survive

WOLFGANG AMADEUS MOZART (1756-1791)

Symphony No 39

New York 22 April 1951	NYPSO	LP: Off-the-Air Record Club OTA 8 CD: As-Disc AS 544 CD: NotaBlu 935.10512 CD: Discantus (Greece) 189 6182

Piano Concerto No 16

New York 23 October 1955	NYPSO Serkin	LP: Movimento musica 01.007 CD: Hunt CDLSMH 34008/CDMP 408 CD: As-Disc AS 511 CD: Notes PGP 11014 CD: Legends LGD 151 CD: Discantus (Greece) 189 6152

Piano Concerto No 20

Florence 17 June 1953	Maggio musicale Orchestra Michelangeli	LP: Cetra DOC 64 CD: Hunt CD 552/CDHP 552 CD: Discantus (Greece) 189 6162

Piano Concerto No 22

New York 6 November 1955	NYPSO Scarpini	CD: As-Disc AS 629 CD: Discantus (Greece) 189 6162

Piano Concerto No 25

New York 23 October 1955	NYPSO Serkin	LP: Movimento musica 01.007 CD: Hunt CDLSMH 34008/CDMP 408 CD: As-Disc AS 511 CD: Notes PGP 11014 CD: Legends LGD 151 CD: Discantus (Greece) 189 6152

SALZBURGER FESTSPIELE 1958

ACHTES ORCHESTER-KONZERT

DIE WIENER PHILHARMONIKER

UNTER DER LEITUNG VON

DIMITRI MITROPOULOS

Solist:

ZINO FRANCESCATTI

Violine

SALZBURGER FESTSPIELE 1957

ELEKTRA

TRAGÖDIE IN EINEM AUFZUGE
VON HUGO VON HOFMANNSTHAL

MUSIK VON
RICHARD STRAUSS

DIRIGENT:
DIMITRI MITROPOULOS

INSZENIERUNG:
HERBERT GRAF

BÜHNENBILD:
GUSTAV VARGO

KOSTÜME:
ANDREAS NOMIKOS

ORCHESTER:
DIE WIENER PHILHARMONIKER
CHOR DER WIENER STAATSOPER

Concerto for two pianos and orchestra

Philadelphia 21 September 1945	Philadelphia Orchestra Vronsky, Babin	78: Columbia (USA) M 628 78: Columbia (Switzerland) DZX 31-33 LP: Columbia (USA) ML 4098 Orchestra described for this recording as Robin Hood Dell Orchestra
New York 13 November 1955	NYPSO Robert & Gaby Casadesus	CD: As-Disc AS 544 CD: NotaBlu 935.10512 CD: Discantus (Greece) 189 6182

Violin Concerto No 3

New York 18 December 1949	NYPSO Szigeti	LP: Discocorp RR 532 CD: As-Disc AS 518 CD: Legends LGD 135 CD: Music and Arts CD 668
New York 2 February 1958	NYPSO Kogan	CD: Discantus (Greece) 189 6172

Violin Concerto No 5

New York 1 January 1956	NYPSO D.Oistrakh	CD: Hunt CDLSMH 34018/CDMP 418 CD: As-Disc AS 502 CD: Discantus (Greece) 189 6172

Divertimento No 2

New York 3 February 1957	NYPSO	CD: Discantus (Greece) 189 6182

Don Giovanni

Salzburg 24 July 1956	VPO Vienna Opera Chorus Grümmer, Streich, Della Casa, Simoneau, Siepi, Corena, Berry, Frick	LP: Replica ARPL 42422 LP: Discoreale DR 10021-10023 CD: Hunt CD 552/CDHP 552 CD: Sony SM3K 64263 Early pressings of CD 552 contained a 1960 performance conducted by Karajan and with a different cast

Idomeneo, overture arranged by Busoni

New York 28 December 1941	NYPSO	CD: As-Disc AS 502 CD: Documents LV 976 CD: Discantus (Greece) 189 6172

Le nozze di Figaro, overture

New York 12 April 1953	NYPSO	CD: As-Disc AS 502 CD: Documents LV 976 CD: Discantus (Greece) 189 6172

Thamos König von Aegypten, entr'actes 1 and 2

Minneapolis 3 December 1940	Minneapolis SO	78: Columbia (USA) 11578D 78: Columbia LX 930 78: Columbia (Australia) LOX 520 78: Columbia (Argentina) 266285 78: Columbia (Brazil) 30-5284 LP: Nickson NH 1001 CD: Nickson NN 1005 Entr'acte No 1 only CD: Sony SSK 6368/MXK 62817

Die Zauberflöte, overture

New York 9 December 1945	NBC SO	CD: Hunt CD 552/CDHP 552 CD: Discantus (Greece) 189 6152
New York 2 February 1958	NYPSO	CD: As-Disc AS 502/AS 544 CD: Documents LV 976 CD: Discantus (Greece) 189 6172

MODEST MUSSORGSKY (1839-1881)

Boris Godunov, abridged version

New York 5-7 March 1956	Metropolitan Opera Orchestra & Chorus Rankin, Hurley, Costa, Kullmann, Tozzi, Scott Sung in English	LP: Book of the Month Club MO 417 LP: Victor LM 6063
New York 10 March 1956	Metropolitan Opera Orchestra & Chorus Thebom, Hurley, Gari, Kullmann, London, Tozzi Sung in English	Unpublished Met broadcast

Night on Bare Mountain, arranged by Rimsky-Korsakov

New York 11 November 1957	NYPSO	LP: Columbia (USA) ML 5335/MS 6044/ 3216 0228/ST 164/4256 CD: Sony MPK 45685

JACQUES OFFENBACH (1819-1880)

Orfée aux enfers, overture

Minneapolis 6 April 1942	Minneapolis SO	Columbia unpublished Recording incomplete

HARILAOS PERPESSAS (1907-1995)

Christus Symphony

New York 3 December 1950	NYPSO	LP: Musica viva (Greece) CD: Discantus (Greece) 189 6092

FRANCIS POULENC (1899-1963)

Concerto for 2 pianos and orchestra

New York 15 December 1947	RCA Victor Orchestra Whittemore, Lowe	78: Victor M 1235 45: Victor WDM 1235 LP: Victor LM 1048

SERGEI PROKOFIEV (1891-1953)

Symphony No 1 "Classical"

Minneapolis 10 January 1940	Minneapolis SO	78: Columbia (USA) X 166 78: Columbia LX 923-924 78: Columbia (Italy) GQX 11259-11260 78: Columbia (Australia) LOX 487-488 LP: Columbia (USA) RL 3021 CD: Nickson NN 1004

Symphony No 5

Munich 9 July 1954	Bavarian RO	LP: Rococo 2082 CD: Orfeo C204 891A
Seattle 8 May 1955	NYPSO	CD: As-Disc AS 525

Piano Concerto No 3

New York 16 December 1945	NBC SO Mitropoulos, piano	CD: As-Disc AS 512
Philadelphia 26 July 1946	Philadelphia Orchestra Mitropoulos, piano	78: Columbia (USA) M 667 LP: Columbia (USA) ML 4389 Orchestra described for this recording as Robin Hood Dell Orchestra
New York 9 August 1949	NYPSO Mitropoulos, piano	LP: New York Philharmonic NYP 85

Violin Concerto No 1

New York 26 February 1956	NYPSO Stern	CD: As-Disc AS 501
New York 27 February 1956	NYPSO Stern	LP: Columbia (USA) ML 5243/MP 39771 LP: Philips CFL 1036 LP: CBS 72203 CD: Sony SM3K 45956

Violin Concerto No 2

New York 27 October 1952	NYPSO Francescatti	LP: Columbia (USA) ML 4648 CD: Sony MH2K 62339
New York 29 April 1956	NYPSO Francescatti	Unpublished radio broadcast

Lieutenant Kije, suite

New York 9 January 1956	NYPSO	LP: Columbia (USA) ML 5101/P 14202 CD: Sony (Greece) awaiting publication

Scythian Suite

New York 27 February 1955	NYPSO	CD: As-Disc AS 525

Overture on Hebrew themes

New York 1950	NYPSO soloists	LP: Decca (USA) DL 8511 LP: Brunswick AXTL 1054 LP: Chronicle of Music DCM 3215 LP: Compagne internationale du disque CID 273045

Romeo and Juliet, ballet suite

New York 3 November 1957	NYPSO	Unpublished radio broadcast
New York 11 November 1957	NYPSO	LP: Columbia (USA) ML 5267/MS 6023/ 3216 0037/3216 0038 LP: Philips ABL 3236/835 517AY LP: CBS 38772/60279 CD: Sony MPK 45557/MPK 46414 Excerpts LP: Columbia (USA) 6P-6209 CD: Sony ASK 5633/MLK 69249/ SBK 48169/SXZK 62589

Quintet for oboe, clarinet, violin, viola and bass

New York 1950	NYPSO soloists	LP: Decca (USA) DL 8511 LP: Brunswick AXTL 1054 LP: Chronicle of Music DCM 3215 LP: Compagne internationale du disque CID 273045

GIACOMO PUCCINI (1858-1924)

La fanciulla del West

Florence 15 June 1954	Teatro Communale Orchestra & Chorus Steber, Del Monaco, Guelfi	LP: Cetra LO 64/DOC 41 CD: Hunt CD 565/CDHP 565 CD: Discantus (Greece) 189 6432 Excerpts LP: Di Stefano GDS 4001 LP: Melodram MEL 675 CD: Foyer CF 2041

Gianni Schicchi

New York 8 February 1958	Metropolitan Opera Orchestra Hurley, Votipka, Anthony, Corena	Unpublished Met broadcast

Madama Butterfly

New York 10-13 December 1956	Metropolitan Opera Orchestra & Chorus Kirsten, Miller, Barioni, Harvuot	LP: Book of the Month Club MO 722 CD: Theorema TH 121.167-121.168 Abridged version
New York 15 December 1956	Metropolitan Opera Orchestra & Chorus Albanese, Elias, Barioni, Brownlee	LP: Movimento musica 03.027 CD: Awaiting publication
New York 29 March 1958	Metropolitan Opera Orchestra & Chorus Stella, Roggero, Fernandi, Harvuot	Unpublished Met broadcast
New York 16 April 1960	Metropolitan Opera Orchestra & Chorus Kirsten, Roggero, Fernandi, Sereni	LP: Readers' Digest RDIS 132/6-8

Manon Lescaut

New York 31 March 1956	Metropolitan Opera Orchestra & Chorus Albanese, Björling,Guarrera, Corena	LP: Morgan MOR 5601 LP: Cetra DOC 9 CD: Melodram CDM 27502

Manon Lescaut, intermezzo

Philadelphia 26 July 1946	Philadelphia Orchestra	78: Columbia (USA) MX 317 45: Columbia (USA) AL 1637/A409 528E LP: Columbia (USA) ML 2053 Orchestra described for this recording as Robin Hood Dell Orchestra

Tosca

Place / Date	Performers	Issues
New York 8 December 1955	Metropolitan Opera Orchestra & Chorus Tebaldi, Tucker, Warren	LP: Metropolitan Opera MET 10 LP: Paragon DSV 52003 This was not a Met broadcast Excerpts LP: Metropolitan Opera MET 408 CD: Hunt CDMP 463 CD: Opera italiana OPI 5
New York 7 January 1956	Metropolitan Opera Orchestra & Chorus Tebaldi, Tucker, Warren	LP: Historical Operatic Treasures ERR 143 LP: Cetra DOC 7 LP: Readers' Digest RDB 132/9-10 CD: Foyer CDE 1003 Excerpts LP: Gioielli della lirica GML 17 CD: Memories HR 4235-4236
New York April 1956	Metropolitan Opera Orchestra & Chorus Milanov,Björling, Cassel	Unpublished private recording This was not a Met broadcast
New York 23 March 1957	Metropolitan Opera Orchestra & Chorus Albanese, Barioni, Warren	Unpublished Met broadcast Excerpts CD: Phoenix PX 5082
New York March 1957	Metropolitan Opera Orchestra & Chorus Kirsten, Barioni, Guarrera	LP: Book of the Month Club MO 724
New York 15 March 1958	Metropolitan Opera Orchestra & Chorus Stella, Tucker, Warren	Unpublished Met broadcast Excerpts CD: Phoenix PX 5082
New York 21 November 1959	Metropolitan Opera Orchestra & Chorus Curtis-Verna, Björling, MacNeil	LP: Ed Smith UORC 148 Excerpts CD: Myto MCD 91647
New York 19 March 1960	Metropolitan Opera Orchestra & Chorus Milanov, Fernandi, Cassel	Unpublished Met broadcast

MINNEAPOLIS SYMPHONY ORCHESTRA

Thirty-fifth Season, 1937–1938

DIMITRI MITROPOULOS
Conductor

DANIELE AMFITHEATROF
Associate Conductor

Twelfth Evening Concert

THURSDAY EVENING, FEBRUARY 24, 1938, AT 8:30

MITROPOULOS, *Conductor*

Soloist: JASCHA HEIFETZ, *Violinist*

PROGRAM

1 Air, from Suite No. 3, in D major - - - - - - *Bach*

2 String Quartet in C-sharp minor, Op. 131 - - *Beethoven*

Performed by String Orchestra

Adagio, ma non troppo e molto espressivo —
Allegro molto vivace —
Allegro moderato —
Andante ma non troppo e molto cantabile —
Presto —
Adagio quasi un poco andante —
Allegro.

(Played without pause)

First Performance in Minneapolis by Orchestra

INTERMISSION

3 Concerto for Violin and Orchestra, in D major,
Op. 61 - - - - - - - - - - - - *Beethoven*

I. Allegro ma non troppo
II. Larghetto
III. Rondo: Allegro molto

(The Rondo follows the Larghetto without pause)

Next Sunday Concert, February 27, *at 5:00 P. M.*
Next Symphony Concert, FRIDAY, March 4, at 8:30 P. M.

HINDEMITH: Sonata for Oboe and Piano

COLUMBIA MASTERWORKS Lp

Harold Gomberg, Oboe Dimitri Mitropoulos, Piano

LOEFFLER: Two Rhapsodies for Oboe, Viola and Piano

Harold Gomberg, Oboe Dimitri Mitropoulos, Piano Milton Katims, Viola

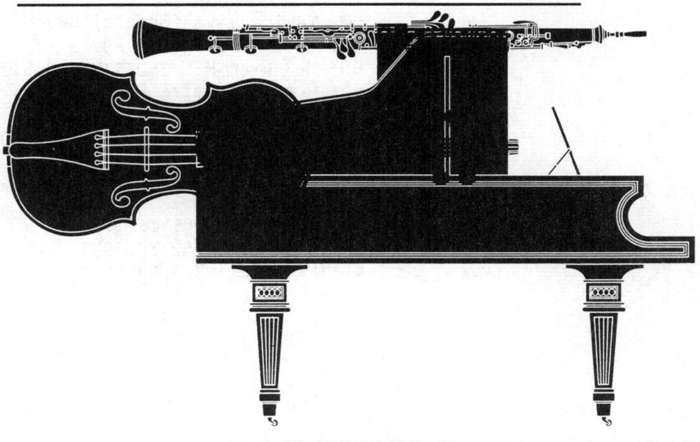

RL 3021

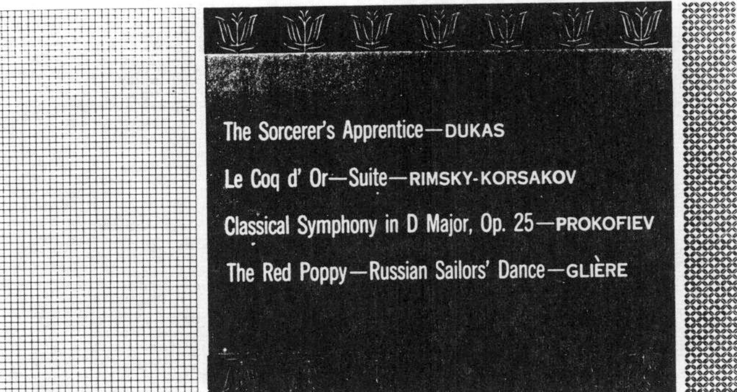

Dimitri Mitropoulos CONDUCTING THE

Minneapolis Symphony Orchestra

Tosca, Act 2 abridged

New York 25 November 1956	Metropolitan Opera Orchestra Callas, London	LP: Voce 13 LP: Melodram MEL 079 LP: Great Operatic Performances GFC 008-009 LP: Musica viva (Greece) 88020 CD: Hunt CD 537/CDHP 537 CD: Melodram MEL 26011/MEL 36513 CD: Great Operatic Performances GOP 714 CD: Foyer CDE 3001 CD: Gala GL 316/GL 100.515/GL 100.526 CD: Classic Options CD 3501 VHS Video: Bel canto Society BCS 0197 Vissi d'arte LP: Dei della musica 13 LP: Joker SM 1282/SM 1353 CD: Memories HR 4293-4294

HENRI RABAUD (1873-1949)

La procession nocturne, symphonic poem

New York 23 January 1950	NYPSO	LP: Columbia (USA) ML 2170 LP: Philips A01604R

SERGEI RACHMANINOV (1873-1943)

Symphony No 2

New York 30 July 1944	NYPSO	Unpublished radio broadcast
Minneapolis 19-20 January 1947	Minneapolis SO	78: Victor M 1148 LP: Victor LM 1068 CD: Nickson NN 1006
New York 2 May 1954	NYPSO	CD: As-Disc AS 524

Piano Concerto No 3

New York 19 February 1956	NYPSO Malcuzynski	Unpublished radio broadcast

Piano Concerto No 4

New York 25 April 1954	NYPSO Hambro	Unpublished radio broadcast

The Isle of the Dead

New York 30 July 1944	NYPSO	Unpublished radio broadcast
Minneapolis 2 March 1945	Minneapolis SO	78: Columbia (USA) M 599 78: Columbia (Canada) D 144 LP: Columbia (USA) ML 4196/P 14151 CD: Nickson NN 1006 CD: Sony MHK 62342

Vocalise

New York 27 February 1955	NYPSO	Unpublished radio broadcast
Seattle 8 May 1955	NYPSO	CD: As-Disc AS 524

Symphonic Dances

New York 20 December 1942	NYPSO	Unpublished radio broadcast
New York 29 June 1950	NYPSO	Unpublished radio broadcast

MAURICE RAVEL (1875-1937)

Piano Concerto in G

New York 29 November 1953	NYPSO Henriot-Schweitzer	Unpublished radio broadcast

Le tombeau de Couperin

Minneapolis 6-7 December 1941	Minneapolis SO	78: Columbia (USA) 19006-19007D LP: Columbia (USA) ML 2032 CD: Nickson NN 1004 CD: Dante LYS 211 CD: Discantus (Greece) 189 6232

Pièce en forme de Habanera, arranged for cello and orchestra by Chardon

Minneapolis 2 March 1945	Minneapolis SO Chardon	78: Columbia (USA) 13104D CD: Nickson NN 1002 CD: Dante LYS 211

NIKOLAI RIMSKY-KORSAKOV (1844-1908)

Le coq d'or, suite

Minneapolis 2 March 1945	Minneapolis SO	78: Columbia (USA) X 254 LP: Columbia (USA) RL 3021 CD: Nickson NN 1007 This recording omits King Dodon on the Battlefield

Bridal Procession (Le coq d'or)

Minneapolis 3 December 1940	Minneapolis SO	78: Columbia (USA) X 212/12899D 78: Columbia (Argentina) 266003 CD: Nickson NN 1003

GIOACHINO ROSSINI (1792-1868)

Il barbiere di Siviglia, excerpt (Largo al factotum)

New York 1950	NBC SO Merrill	LP: Voice of America CD: Nickson NN 1008-1009

ANTON RUBINSTEIN (1829-1894)

Piano Concerto No 4

New York 31 March 1952	NYPSO Levant	LP: Columbia (USA) ML 4599/3216 0169 CD: Palladio PD 4132

CAMILLE SAINT-SAENS (1835-1921)

Symphony No 2

New York 2 March 1952	NYPSO	Unpublished radio broadcast

Piano Concerto No 2

New York 19 April 1953	NYPSO Rubinstein	CD: As-Disc AS 508 CD: Music and Arts CD 655 CD: Legends LGD 107 CD: Discantus (Greece) 189 6292

Cello Concerto No 1

New York 21 April 1951	NYPSO Rose	LP: Columbia (USA) ML 4425/P 14167

Violin Concerto No 3

New York 23 January 1950	NYPSO Francescatti	78: Columbia (USA) MM 937 78: Columbia LX 1526-1528 LP: Columbia (USA) ML 4315/MS 6268 LP: Columbia (France) FCX 140 LP: Philips SBL 5219 LP: CBS 72151/73143/78211 LP: Supraphon SUA 10935/SUAST 10935 CD: Sony MPK 46728/SMK 53085/MH2K 62339

Introduction and rondo capriccioso for violin and orchestra

New York 29 December 1940	NYPSO Spalding	Unpublished radio broadcast

Danse macabre, symphonic poem

New York 27 November 1950	NYPSO	78: Columbia (USA) 13150D 45: Philips ABE 10008 /A409 013E LP: Columbia (USA) ML 2170/ML 5154/ AAL 8/P 14205 LP: Philips A01604R

La jeunesse d'Hercule, symphonic poem

New York 6 January 1956	NYPSO	LP: Columbia (USA) ML 5154/P 14205

Phaeton, symphonic poem

New York 9 January 1956	NYPSO	LP: Columbia (USA) ML 5154/P 14205 CD: Sony ASK 5633/SX2K 62587

Le rouet d'Omphale, symphonic poem

New York 23 January 1950	NYPSO	78: Columbia 13151D 45: Philips ABE 10008/A409 013E LP: Columbia (USA) ML 2170/ML 5154/AAL 8 P 14205 LP: Philips A01604R

FRANZ SCHMIDT (1874-1939)

Symphony No 2

Vienna 28 August 1958	VPO	CD: Music and Arts CD 991

Das Buch mit 7 Siegeln

Salzburg 23 August 1959	VPO Singverein Güden, Malaniuk, Dermota, Berry, Wunderlich	LP: Melodram MEL 705 CD: Melodram MEL 27078 CD: Sony SM2K 68442 Excerpts CD: Verona 28044-28045

ARTUR SCHNABEL (1882-1951)

Symphony

Minneapolis 13 December 1946	Minneapolis SO	Unpublished radio broadcast Incomplete recording of world premiere performance

ARNOLD SCHOENBERG (1874-1951)

Orchestral variations

Salzburg 21 August 1960	BPO	CD: Nuova era 013.6306
Cologne 24 October 1960	WDR Orchestra	CD: Hunt CDGI 753

Verklärte Nacht

New York 3 March 1958	NYPSO	LP: Columbia (USA) ML 5285/MS 6007/ 3216 0298
Vienna 28 August 1958	VPO	CD: Music and Arts CD 991

Pelleas und Melisande

New York 29 October 1953	NYPSO	CD: Music and Arts CD 967

Violin Concerto

New York 1 December 1952	NYPSO Krassner	LP: Columbia (USA) ML 4857
Munich 9 July 1954	Bavarian RO Krassner	CD: Orfeo C204 891A
Cologne 16 July 1954	WDR Orchestra Krassner	LP: Gunmar Music GM 2006 CD: Gunmar Music GM 2006

Piano Concerto

New York 3 April 1958	NYPSO Gould	CD: Nuova era 013.6306 CD: Memories HR 4415-4416

Erwartung

New York 18 November 1951	NYPSO Dow	CD: As-Disc AS 541
New York 19 November 1951	NYPSO Dow	LP: Columbia (USA) ML 4524 LP: Philips ABL 3393 CD: Sony MH2K 62759 First commercial recording of the work

Serenade for baritone and septet

New York December 1949	ISCM members Galjour	LP: Counterpoint Esoteric 501M/ 5501S/MC 20005 LP: Concert Hall CM 2175 First commercial recording of the work

String Quartet No 2

New York 23 December 1945	NBC SO members Varnay	Unpublished radio broadcast

FRANZ SCHUBERT (1797-1828)

Symphony No 2

Boston 23 December 1944	Boston SO	Unpublished radio broadcast

GUNTHER SCHULLER (Born 1925)

Symphony for brass and percussion

New York 14 June 1956	Brass ensemble of Jazz & Classical Music Society, whose members include Schuller	LP: Columbia (USA) CL 941 CD: Sony SRCS 5696/CK 64929 World premiere recording

ROBERT SCHUMANN (1810-1856)

Symphony No 1 "Spring"

New York 8 January 1950	NYPSO	Unpublished radio broadcast
New York 15 November 1953	NYPSO	CD: As-Disc AS 627 CD: Discantus (Greece) 189 6242
New York 11 November 1956	NYPSO	CD: As-Disc AS 501

Symphony No 2

Minneapolis 3 December 1940	Minneapolis SO	78: Columbia (USA) M 503 LP: Columbia (USA) ML 3025 CD: Nickson NN 1008-1009 CD: Grammofono AB 78646-78649 CD: Iron Needle IN 1327 CD: Dante LYS 152 CD: Discantus (Greece) 189 6202
Athens October 1955	NYPSO	Unpublished radio broadcast

Symphony No 3 "Rhenish"

Minneapolis 20 January 1947	Minneapolis SO	78: Victor M 1184 45: Victor WDM 1184 LP: Victor LM 1067/LBC 1058 CD: Nickson NN 1007 CD: Dante LYS 152

Piano Concerto

New York 21 November 1948	NYPSO Michelangeli	LP: Rococo 2024 LP: Arioso 15006 CD: As-Disc AS 321 CD: Historical Performances HP 21 CD: Notes PGP 11027 Michelangeli's US debut performance
New York 10 February 1952	NYPSO Hess	CD: Melodram MEL 18024 CD: As-Disc AS 627 CD: Discantus (Greece) 189 6242

Overture, scherzo and finale

New York 11 March 1951	NYPSO	CD: As-Disc AS 627 CD: Discantus (Greece) 189 6242

ALEXANDER SCRIABIN (1872-1915)

Poème de l'extase

New York 20 March 1953	NYPSO	LP: Columbia (USA) ML 4731/P 14184 CD: Theorema TH 121.132 CD: Sony (Greece) awaiting publication
New York 19 April 1953	NYPSO	CD: As-Disc AS 508 CD: Legends LGD 107 CD: Discantus (Greece) 189 6222

Prometheus

New York 20 March 1953	NYPSO Westminster Choir Hambro	LP: Columbia (USA) ML 4731/P 14184 CD: Sony (Greece) awaiting publication
New York 9 April 1953	NYPSO	CD: Music and Arts CD 967

ROGER SESSIONS (1896-1988)

Symphony No 2

New York 15 January 1950	NYPSO	Unpublished radio broadcast
New York 16 January 1950	NYPSO	78: Columbia (USA) MM 920 LP: Columbia (USA) ML 2120/ML 4784 LP: Composers' Recordings SD 278 CD: Composers' Recordings CRICD 573 World premiere recording

GORDON SHERWOOD (Born 1929)

Introduction and allegro

New York 5 May 1957	NYPSO	CD: As-Disc AS 543

DIMITRI SHOSTAKOVICH (1906-1975)

Symphony No 5

New York 1 December 1952	NYPSO	LP: Columbia (USA) ML 4739/P 14185 CD: Theorema TH 121.151 CD: Sony (Greece) awaiting publication

Symphony No 10

New York 18 October 1954	NYPSO	LP: Columbia (USA) ML 4959/3216 0123 LP: Philips ABL 3052/A01175L LP: CBS 61457 CD: Sony MPK 45698
Athens 2 October 1955	NYPSO	CD: Hellas (Greece) YPPO 2

Violin Concerto No 1

New York 1 January 1956	NYPSO D.Oistrakh	LP: Cetra DOC 6 US premiere performance
New York 2 January 1956	NYPSO D.Oistrakh	LP: Columbia (USA) ML 5077/MP 39771 LP: Philips ABL 3101 LP: CBS 77394 CD: Sony CD 39771

JEAN SIBELIUS (1865-1957)

Violin Concerto

New York March 1951	NYPSO Heifetz	CD: Music and Arts CD 766 CD: As-Disc AS 622 CD: Legends LGD 128

YORGOS SICILIANOS (Born 1920)

Symphony No 1

New York 1 March 1958	NYPSO	LP: Archio PSI 91065 CD: Lyra CD 0074 World premiere performance

ELIE SIEGMEISTER (Born 1909)

Ozark Set, orchestral suite

Minneapolis 2 March 1945	Minneapolis SO	78: Columbia (USA) X 262 LP: Columbia (USA) ML 2123 LP: Orion ORS 73116 CD: Nickson NN 1005 World premiere recording
New York 23 December 1945	NBC SO	Unpublished radio broadcast

NIKOS SKALKOTTAS (1904-1949)

4 Greek dances

Athen 1 October 1955	NYPSO	CD: Hellas (Greece) YPPO 1
New York 9 January 1956	NYPSO	45: Columbia (USA) BA 307001 45: Philips AE 409152 LP: Columbia (USA) ML 5335 CD: Nickson NN 1010 CD: Sony SXK 62718

RICHARD STRAUSS (1864-1949)

Elektra

New York 25 December 1949	NYPSO Varnay, Jessner, Nikolaidi, Jagel, Janssen	LP: Robin Hood RHR 5101-5102 LP: Off-the-Air Record Club OTA 4 CD: Arlecchino ARL 20-22 Arlecchino incorrectly dated January 1949
Florence 16-18 May 1950	Maggio musicale Orchestra A.Konetzni, Mödl, Ilitsch, Klarwein, Braun	LP: Cetra CS 1209/CS 519-520/ LPO 2010/TRV 7 LP: Rococo 50039 LP: Everest S 459 LP: Turnabout THS 65040-65041 CD: Cetra 9075.137/CDO 4 CD: PRSR 158-159 PRSR 158-159 incorrectly described as a performance in Vienna
Salzburg 7 August 1957	VPO Borkh, Della Casa, Madeira, Lorenz, Böhme	LP: Cetra LO 83 LP: Concert EMAM 701 LP: Discocorp SID 731 CD: Nuova era NE 2241-2242 CD: Memories HR 4380-4381 CD: Orfeo C456 972I
New York 6 March 1958	NYPSO Borkh, Thebom, Yeend, D.Lloyd, Tozzi	CD: Hunt CDMP 459

Elektra, excerpt (Weh, ganz allein!)

Cologne 7 September 1959	WDR Orchestra Varnay	LP: Estro armonico EA 035 LP: Cetra DOC 13 CD: Hunt CD 581/CDHP 581

Salome

New York 8 January 1955	Metropolitan Opera Orchestra Goltz, Thebom, Sullivan, Vinay, Schöffler	LP: Hope Records HOPE 238 Excerpts CD: Hunt CDMP 459
New York 8 February 1958	Metropolitan Opera Orchestra Borkh, Thebom, Gari, Vinay, Harrell	LP: Cetra LO 82 CD: Hunt CDMP 459

Salome, Dance of the 7 veils

New York 3 November 1956	NYPSO	LP: Columbia (USA) ML 5198

Eine Alpensinfonie

Venice 19 September 1956	VPO	CD: Hunt CD 581/CDHP 581

Also sprach Zarathustra

Salzburg 10 August 1958	Concertgebouw Orchestra	CD: Orfeo C458 971B
Cologne 7 September 1959	WDR Orchestra	LP: Cetra DOC 13 CD: Hunt CD 508/CDHP 508 CD: Virtuoso 269.7032

Burleske for piano and orchestra

New York 9 February 1958	NYPSO Serkin	CD: Hunt CD 581/CDHP 581

Don Juan

New York 28 October 1956	NYPSO	CD: Hunt CD 581/CDHP 581

Don Quixote

Cologne 7 September 1959	WDR Orchestra Bauer	LP: Cetra DOC 13 CD: Hunt CD 508/CDHP 508

Die Frau ohne Schatten, symphonic fantasy

New York 11 February 1954	NYPSO	CD: Hunt CD 581/CDHP 581 CD: As-Disc AS 622 CD: Legends LGD 128

Sinfonia domestica

New York April 1950	NYPSO	CD: Hunt CD 583/CDHP 583
Cologne 19 July 1957	WDR Orchestra	CD: Hunt CD 581/CDHP 581

Tod und Verklärung

New York 2 December 1956	NYPSO	LP: New York Philharmonic NYP 88 CD: Hunt CD 583/CDHP 583 CD: As-Disc AS 622 CD: Legends LGD 128

IGOR STRAVINSKY (1882-1971)

Petrushka, 1911 version

New York 5 March 1951	NYPSO	LP: Columbia (USA) ML 4438/P 14169 LP: Philips ABL 2037/GBR 6519/ A01104L/S06641R

L'histoire du soldat

New York 21 May 1948	Instrumentalists Anderson, Voland, Bittner, Van den Berg	Unpublished radio broadcast

HOWARD SWANSON (1907-1978)

Night music

New York 1950	NYPSO members	LP: Decca (USA) DL 8511 LP: Brunswick AXTL 1054 LP: Chronicle of Music DCM 3215 LP: Compagne internationale du disque 273045

ROY TRAVIS (Born 1922)

Symphonic Allegro

New York 4 January 1952	NYPSO	LP: Columbia (USA) AAL 16

METROPOLITAN OPERA

SEASON 1957-1958

Thursday Evening, April 3, 1958, at 8:15

(Subscription Performance)

NEW PRODUCTION

MADAMA BUTTERFLY

Opera in three acts
Libretto by Luigi Illica and Giuseppe Giacosa
Music by Giacomo Puccini

Conductor: Dimitri Mitropoulos — Staged by Yoshio Aoyama

Sets and Costumes by Motohiro Nagasaka
Supervisory Scenic Designer: Charles Elson
Supervisory Costume Designer: Ming Cho Lee

Cio-Cio-San .... Victoria de los Angeles
B. F. Pinkerton .... Carlo Bergonzi
U. S. Consul Sharpless .... Frank Guarrera
Suzuki .... Margaret Roggero
Kate Pinkerton .... Madelaine Chambers
Goro .... Alessio De Paolis
Yamadori .... George Cehanovsky
The uncle-priest .... Norman Scott
The Imperial Commissary .... Calvin Marsh

Chorus Master...... Kurt Adler
Associate Chorus Master......Leo Mueller
Musical Preparation......Corrado Muccini

The new production of MADAMA BUTTERFLY was made possible by a generous and deeply appreciated gift of Mr. Cornelius V. Starr.

KNABE PIANO USED EXCLUSIVELY

Program continued on the next page

THE AUDIENCE IS RESPECTFULLY, BUT URGENTLY, REQUESTED NOT TO INTERRUPT THE MUSIC WITH APPLAUSE.

SALZBURGER FESTSPIELE 1960

40 JAHRE SALZBURGER FESTSPIELE

NEUNTES ORCHESTER-KONZERT

GUSTAV MAHLER

VIII. SINFONIE

für Soli, Chor, Orchester und Orgel

Solisten

MIMI COERTSE, Sopran
HILDE ZADEK, Sopran
LUCRETIA WEST, Alt
IRA MALANIUK, Alt
GIUSEPPE ZAMPIERI, Tenor
HERMANN PREY, Bariton
OTTO EDELMANN, Baß

DIRIGENT
DIMITRI MITROPOULOS

DIE WIENER PHILHARMONIKER
KONZERTVEREINIGUNG WIENER STAATSOPERNCHOR
SINGVEREIN DER GESELLSCHAFT DER MUSIKFREUNDE WIEN
DIE WIENER SÄNGERKNABEN

PIOTR TCHAIKOVSKY (1840-1893)

Symphony No 2 "Little Russian"

Minneapolis 10-11 March 1946	Minneapolis SO	78: Columbia (USA) M 673 LP: Columbia (USA) ML 4252/RL 6623/ P 14158 CD: Nickson NN 1010 CD: Discantus (Greece) 189 6322

Symphony No 4

Minneapolis 10 January- 26 November 1940	Minneapolis SO	78: Columbia (USA) M 468 LP: Columbia (USA) RL 3007 CD: Grammofono AB 78608/AB 78646-78649 CD: Palladio PD 4104 CD: Legends LGD 147 CD: Discantus (Greece) 189 6322 Palladio and Legends incorrectly describe orchestra as New York Philharmonic

Symphony No 5

New York 27 March 1954	NYPSO	LP: Columbia (USA) ML 5075/CL 764/ P 14199 LP: Philips SBL 5205/GBL 5631/ S04605L CD: Sony (Greece) awaiting publication

Symphony No 6 "Pathétique"

New York 11 November 1957	NYPSO	LP: Columbia (USA) ML 5235/MS 6006/ ST 164/3216 0216 LP: Philips A01366L/SABL 104 CD: Sony MPK 45699 Excerpt LP: Columbia (USA) SF 1

Piano Concerto No 1

Minneapolis 16 November 1947	Minneapolis SO Rubinstein	78: Victor M 1159 45: Victor WDM 1159 LP: Victor LM 1028/VLS 45502 LP: HMV (France) FALP 275 CD: Palladio PD 4132
New York 11 November 1956	NYPSO Xydis-Antoniades	Unpublished radio broadcast

Violin Concerto

New York 27 March 1954	NYPSO Francescatti	LP: Columbia (USA) ML 4965 LP: Philips ABL 3159/A01214L/A01615R LP: CBS 72305 CD: Sony MH2K 62339 Excerpt LP: Columbia (USA) D 2 LP: Philips GBL 5534

Suite No 1

New York 18 October- 17 November 1954	NYPSO	LP: Columbia (USA) ML 4966/P 14195 LP: Philips ABL 3079/A01160L This recording omits third movement

Capriccio italien

New York 22 April 1957	NYPSO	LP: Columbia (USA) ML 5335/MS 6044/ 3216 0228 LP: CBS 4256/73143/78211 CD: Flowers BL 022 CD: Sony MPK 45699/ASK 5633/SX2K 62587

Marche slave

New York 11 November 1957	NYPSO	LP: Columbia (USA) ML 5335/MS 6044/ 3216 0228 LP: CBS 4256 CD: Flowers BL 022 CD: Sony MPK 45699

Evgeny Onegin

New York 7 December 1957	Metropolitan Opera Orchestra & Chorus Amara, Elias, Lipton, Tucker, London, Tozzi Sung in English	LP: Great Operatic Performances GOP 50 CD: Great Operatic Performances GOP 707
New York December 1957	Metropolitan Opera Orchestra & Chorus Amara, Elias, Lipton, Tucker, Guarrera, Tozzi Sung in English	LP: Book of the Month Club MO 824 Abridged version

RALPH VAUGHAN WILLIAMS (1872-1958)

Symphony No 2 "London"

New York 9 December 1945	NBC SO	Unpublished radio broadcast

Symphony No 4

New York 18 December 1949	NYPSO	Unpublished radio broadcast
New York 9 January 1956	NYPSO	LP: Columbia (USA) ML 5158/CML 5158 LP: Philips ABR 4065 LP: CBS 61432 CD: Sony SMK 58933/SBK 62754

Concerto for 2 pianos and orchestra

New York 17 February 1952	NYPSO Whittemore, Lowe	Unpublished radio broadcast

Fantasia on a theme of Thomas Tallis

Minneapolis 2 March 1945	Minneapolis SO	78: Columbia (USA) MX 300 LP: Columbia (USA) ML 4196/P 14151
New York 3 March 1958	NYPSO	LP: Columbia (USA) ML 5285/MS 6007/ 3216 0298/6P-6209 LP: CBS 73143/78211 CD: Sony SMK 58933/SBK 62754

GIUSEPPE VERDI (1813-1901)

Un ballo in maschera

New York 22 January 1955	Metropolitan Opera Orchestra & Chorus Milanov, Peters, Madeira, Tucker, Metternich	LP: Raritas OPR 408 LP: Cetra LO 4 LP: Foyer FO 1020 CD: Foyer 2CF-2004 Excerpts LP: Gioielli della lirica GML 13
New York 10 December 1955	Metropolitan Opera Orchestra & Chorus Milanov, Peters, Anderson, Peerce, Merrill	CD: Myto MCD 942.100 CD: Discantus (Greece) 189 6472

Un ballo in maschera, highlights

New York 9-21 January 1955	Metropolitan Opera Orchestra Milanov, Peters, Anderson, Peerce, Warren	LP: Victor LM 1911/LM 1932/LM 20146/ VIC 1336/VICS 1336 LP: HMV ALP 1476 LP: Melodiya D 013891 CD: RCA/BMG RG 79112 CD: Theorema TH 121.146 Excerpts LP: RCA RL 85177 CD: RCA/BMG GD 60074/GD 87911/ 09026 615802 CD: Metropolitan Opera MET 107

Ernani

New York 29 December 1956	Metropolitan Opera Orchestra & Chorus Milanov, Del Monaco, Warren, Siepi	LP: MRF Records MRF 6 LP: Cetra LO 12 LP: Foyer FO 1021 LP: Dei della musica DMV 17-19 CD: Foyer 2CF-2006 CD: Hunt CDMP 470 <u>Excerpts</u> LP: Di Stefano GDS 4001 LP: Melodram MEL 675 CD: Virtuoso 269.7132 CD: Foyer CF 2041
Florence 14 June 1957	Teatro communale Orchestra & Chorus Cerquetti, Del Monaco, Bastianini, Christoff	LP: Morgan MOR 5702 LP: Raritas OPR 404 LP: Collectors Limited Editions CLS 51/AMDRL 32814 LP: Cetra DOC 36 CD: Melodram MEL 27016 CD: Discantus (Greece) 189 6452 <u>Excerpts</u> LP: Ed Smith EJS 422 LP: Foyer FO 1035 LP: Joker SM 1299 LP: Gioielli della lirica GML 33 LP: Movimento musica 01.012 CD: Memories HR 4400-4401 CD: Opera italiana OPI 09 CD: Hunt CDMP 470

La forza del destino

Florence 14 June 1953	Teatro communale Orchestra & Chorus Tebaldi, Barbieri, Del Monaco, Protti, Siepi	LP: Morgan MOR 5301 LP: Cetra LO 17 LP: Turnabout THS 65117-65119 LP: Foyer FO 1019 CD: Foyer 3CF-2005 CD: Palladio PD 4210-4212 CD: Discantus (Greece) 189 6352 Excerpts LP: Foyer FO 1035 LP: Joker SM 1297 LP: Gioielli della lirica GML 7 LP: Movimento musica 01.012 CD: Memories HR 4235-4236 CD: Foyer CF 2041
Vienna 23 September 1960	VPO Vienna Opera Chorus Stella, Simionato, Di Stefano, Bastianini, Kreppel	LP: Melodram MEL 023 CD: Di Stefano GDS 31022 Excerpts LP: Joker SM 1298 LP: Phoenix PLE 25514

La forza del destino, overture

Florence 17 June 1953	Maggio musicale Orchestra	LP: Cetra DOC 64
Athens 2 October 1955	NYPSO	CD: Hellas (Greece) YPPO 1

Simon Boccanegra

New York 2 April 1960	Metropolitan Opera Orchestra & Chorus Milanov, Bergonzi, Guarrera, Tozzi, Flagello, Scott	LP: MRF Records MRF 84 LP: Estro armonico EA 023 LP: Foyer FO 1023 CD: Stradivarius STR 10032-10033 CD: Memories HR 4539-4540 CD: Discantus (Greece) 189 6492

I vespri siciliani, overture

New York 16 March 1958	NYPSO	Unpublished radio broadcast

Vittorio, ballet arranged by Burger comprising music mainly taken from Ernani

New York 8 January 1955	Metropolitan Opera Orchestra	Unpublished Met broadcast Performed in a double bill with Salome

GIOVANNI BATTISTA VIOTTI (1755-1824)

Violin Concerto No 22

New York 18 October 1953	NYPSO Menuhin	LP: Rococo 2024

ANTONIO VIVALDI (1678-1741)

Concerto in G minor

New York 13 October 1957	NYPSO	Unpublished radio broadcast

RICHARD WAGNER (1813-1883)

Götterdämmerung, Act 3

New York 30 October 1955	NYPSO Varnay, Amara, Vinay, Harvuot, Vichegonov	CD: As-Disc AS 549 CD: Discantus (Greece) 189 6262 Excerpts CD: NotaBlu 935.1063

Siegfried, Forest murmurs

New York 30 October 1955	NYPSO	CD: As-Disc AS 549 CD: NotaBlu 935.1063 CD: Discantus (Greece) 189 6262

Die Walküre

New York 2 February 1957	Metropolitan Opera Orchestra Harshaw, Schech, Thebom, Vinay, Edelmann, Böhme	LP: Raritas OPR 403 LP: Melodram MEL 004 CD: Nuova era NE 2211-2213 CD: Discantus (Greece) 189 6382

Die Walküre, extracts (Nun zäume dein Ross!; Der alte Sturm, die alte Müh'!; Nimm' den Eid!; Zurück von dem Speer!...to end of Act 2; Wo ist Brünnhild', wo die Verbrecherin?...to end of opera)

New York 11 February- 6 March 1957	Metropolitan Opera Orchestra Harshaw, Schech, Thebom, Vinay, Uhde, Scott	LP: Book of the Month Club MO 728 Farewell & Magic Fire Music LP: Melodram MEL 094

WILLIAM WALTON (1902-1983)

Cello Concerto

New York 5 May 1957	NYPSO Piatigorsky	Unpublished radio broadcast

Portsmouth Point, overture

Minneapolis 10 March 1946	Minneapolis SO	78: Columbia (USA) 12755D LP: Nickson NH 1001 CD: Nickson NN 1004

Belshazzar's Feast

New York 12 May 1957	NYPSO Schola cantorum Tozzi	Unpublished radio broadcast

CARL MARIA VON WEBER (1786-1826)

Der Freischütz, overture

New York 10 October 1954	NYPSO	Unpublished radio broadcast
New York 10 April 1955	NYPSO	Unpublished radio broadcast

Jubel, overture

Minneapolis 11 March 1946	Minneapolis SO	78: Columbia (USA) 12891D LP: Columbia (USA) RL 3038 CD: Nickson NN 1008-1009 CD: Dante LYS 172

ANTON VON WEBERN (1883-1945)

Passacaglia for orchestra

New York 23 January 1960	NYPSO	CD: As-Disc AS 540

JAROMIR WEINBERGER (1896-1967)

Polka and Fugue (Schwanda the Bagpiper)

Minneapolis 20 January 1947	Minneapolis SO	78: Victor 12-0019 45: Victor 49-0287 CD: Nickson NN 1002
New York 2 November 1956	NYPSO	45: Philips A409 094E LP: Columbia (USA) ML 5198/4256

ERMANNO WOLF-FERRARI (1876-1948)

I gioielli della madonna, intermezzi acts 2 and 3

Philadelphia 26 July 1946	Philadelphia Orchestra	78: Columbia (USA) MX 317 45: Columbia (USA) AL 1637/A409 528E 45: Philips SBF 124 LP: Columbia (USA) ML 2053 Orchestra described for this recording as Robin Hood Dell Orchestra

BERND ALOIS ZIMMERMANN (1918-1970)

Oboe Concerto

Cologne 31 August 1959	WDR Orchestra Faber	LP: Cetra DOC 5

Mitropoulos interviews: list compiled by Stathis Arfanis

Minneapolis Farewell Speech. (In English)

Recording Place & Date Minneapolis 18 Mar. 1949 — Radio Broadcast UNPUBLISHED

Rehearsal & Performance excerpts from Liszt's "A Faust Symhony" 3rd Movement - "Mefistofeles" - from the 20th Century Fox film "Of Men and Music". Directed by Irving Reis. 1951 Release. (In English)

Recording Place & Date New York Mar. 1950

Interview in Iowa. (In English)

Recording Place & Date Iowa 1952 — Radio Broadcast UNPUBLISHED

Interview with Jim Fassett on CBS Radio. (In English)

Recording Place & Date New York 1954 — Radio Broadcast UNPUBLISHED

Interview with Lee Eitzen on W.N.C.N. (In English)

Recording Place & Date New York 1954 — Radio Broadcast UNPUBLISHED

"This I Believe" : Interview with Edward R. Murrow. (In English)

Recording Place & Date New York 1954 — Columbia ML ? Ed. R. Murrow Series

Announces the complete programme of this concert, which includes : Forza - Overture, Brahms - Haydn Variations, Skalkottas - Four Greek Dances, Beethoven - Symphony No 3 (In Greek).

Recording Place & Date Athens 2 Oct. 1955 — LP ERT-ERA 15664 CD YPPO 1

Dedicates this performance of the Berlioz - Requiem to the memory of Wilhelm Furtwängler. (In German)

Recording Place & Date Salzburg 15 Aug. 1956 — LP Cetra LO 509 LP Mov. Musica 02.024

See it Now: TV Show, interview on CBS with Edward R. Murrow (In English)

Recording Place & Date New York March, 1957 — Radio Broadcast UNPUBLISHED

Das Musicalische Selbstporträt: Dimitri Mitropoulos. Interview by Joseph Muller-Marien & Hannes Reinhart (In German)

Recording Place & Date N.D.R Hamburg Production, 1959 — Radio Broadcast UNPUBLISHED

The compositions of Dimitri Mitropoulos: list compiled by Stathis Arfanis

"L' Alouette et ces petits", for voice and piano (1920)

Verses from the fable of La Fontaine.

Recording Place & Date	Westchester, N.Y. 18 May 1975	Radio broadcast tape
Soprano	Berenice Bramson	UNPUBLISHED
Piano		

Concerto Grosso (1928)

Recording Place & Date	Athens 28 Nov. 1975	Radio broadcast tape
Orchestra	GRSO	UNPUBLISHED
Conductor	Choo Hoey	
Piano part	Nelly Semitecolo	

Concerto Grosso (1928)

Recording Place & Date	Athens 2 May 1996	Unofficial tape recording
Orchestra	OC	UNPUBLISHED
Conductor	Semion Kogan	
Piano Part	?	

"4 Cytheran Dances" for piano (1926)

Recording Place & Date	Athens 31 Oct. 1996	Radio broadcast tape
Piano	Maria Asteriadou	UNPUBLISHED

"4 Cytheran Dances" for piano (1926)

Premmiere Recording.

Recording Place & Date	Milan 1 to 4 Dec. 1996	CD Agorá AG 099.1
Piano	Danae Kara	

"Dance des Faunes-Scherzo Fantastique", for String Quartet (1915)

Recording Place & Date	Westchester, N.Y. 18 May 1975	Private Recording
1st Violin		UNPUBLISHED
2nd Violin		
Viola		
Cello	Joel Krosnick	

"Dance des Faunes-Scherzo Fantastique", for String Quartet (1915)

Recording Place & Date	Milan 13 Nov. 1993	Private Recording
1st Violin	George Demertjis	UNPUBLISHED
2nd Violin	Dimitris Handrakis	
Viola	Paris Anastasiadis	
Cello	Byron Fidetzis	

"Dance des Faunes-Scherzo Fantastique", for String Quartet (1915)

Recording Place & Date	New York 3 Mar. 1996	Private Recording
1st Violin	George Demertjis	UNPUBLISHED
2nd Violin	Nton Miller	
Viola	Frank Forester	
Cello	Maria Kitsopoulos	

"Dance des Faunes-Scherzo Fantastique", for string quartet (1915)

Recording Place & Date	Athens 31 Oct. 1996	Radio broadcast tape
1st Violin	George Demertjis	UNPUBLISHED
2nd Violin	Dimitris Handrakis	
Viola	Paris Anastasiadis	
Cello	Apostolos Handrakis	

"Douleur", for Voice and Piano

Verses : Unknown

Recording Place & Date	Milan 13 Nov. 1993	Private Recording
Barytone	Louis Manikas	UNPUBLISHED
Piano	Aris Garoufalis	

"Douleur", for Voice and Piano

Verses : Unknown

Recording Place & Date	Athens 3 May 1996	Unofficial Recording
Soprano	Julia Troussa	UNPUBLISHED
Piano	Aliki Vatikioti	

"Douleur", for Voice and Piano

Verses : Unknown

Recording Place & Date	Athens 31 Oct. 1996	Radio broadcast tape
Soprano	Julia Troussa	UNPUBLISHED
Piano	Maria Asteriadou	

"Electra" Scenic Music for Sofocles' Tragedy. (Excerpt)

Recording Place & Date	Athens 1952 ?	LP Philips 6641278
Orchestra	Unknown	CD Philips 526458-2
Conductor	George Lykoudis	

"Electra" Scenic Music for Sofocles' Tragedy

Recording Place & Date	Athens 22, 23 & 26 Oct. 1976	Radio broadcast tape
Orchestra	GRSO	UNPUBLISHED
Conductor	Byron Fidetzis	
Soprano solo	Varvara Gavakou	

"The Entombement", Symphonic Poem (1915)

Recording Place & Date	Athens 8 Nov. 1975	Radio broadcast tape
Orchestra	GRSO	UNPUBLISHED
Conductor	Choo Hoey	

"The Entombement", Symphonic Poem (1915)

Recording Place & Date	Athens Mar. 1979	Private Recording
Orchestra	ASO	UNPUBLISHED
Conductor	Byron Fidetzis	

"The Entombement", Symphonic Poem (1915)

Recording Place & Date	Athens 2 May 1996	Unofficial tape recording
Orchestra	OC	UNPUBLISHED
Conductor	Semion Kogan	

"The Entombement", Symphonic Poem (1915)

Concert to commemorate the 100th anniversary of D. Mitropoulos birth.

Recording Place & Date	Thessaloniki 2 Nov. 1996	Radio broadcast tape
Orchestra	NBSO	UNPUBLISHED
Conductor	Byron Fidetzis	

"Hippolytos" Scenic Music for Euripides' Tragedy

Orchestral parts only. Arrangement by Takis Kalageropoulos for wind instruments and doubble basses

Recording Place & Date	Athens 23 May 1971	Private Recording
Orchestra	Panharmonia	UNPUBLISHED
Conductor	Takis Kalogeropoulos	

"10 Inventions" Song Cycle

Verses : C. P. Cavafy a. Long ago, b. Comes to rest, c.To call up the shades, d. The next table, e. Days of 1903, f. Grey, g. In the street, h. The afternoon sun, I. I' ve looked so much, j. I went.

Recording Place & Date	Athens 22 Jan. 1983	Radio broadcast tape
Soprano	Alexandra Kambouropoulou	UNPUBLISHED
Piano	Yannis Y. Papaioannou	

"4 Inventions" for Voice and Piano[1]

Verses : C. P. Cavafy a. Delight, b. A Night, c. The Begining, d. In Despair. Premmiere Performance.

Recording Place & Date	Athens 11 Oct. 1985	Radio broadcast tape
Soprano	Myrto Douli-Porfyri	UNPUBLISHED
Piano	Aris Garoufalis	

"10 Inventions" Song Cycle

Verses : C. P. Cavafy a. Long ago, b. Comes to rest, c.To call up the shades, d. The next table, e. Days of 1903, f. Grey, g. In the street, h. The afternoon sun, I. I' ve looked so much, j. I went.

Recording Place & Date	Athens 23 Nov. 1990	Radio broadcast tape
Barytone	Spiros Sakkas	UNPUBLISHED
Piano	George Kouroupos	

"10 Inventions" Song Cycle

Verses : C. P. Cavafy a. Long ago, b. Comes to rest, c.To call up the shades, d. The next table, e. Days of 1903, f. Grey, g. In the street, h. The afternoon sun, I. I' ve looked so much, j. I went. Premmiere Recording.

Recording Place & Date	Athens Jul. 1991	LP Mus. Viva MV 88031
Soprano	Lila Adamaki	CD Mus. Viva MV 88031
Piano	Yannis Papadopoulos	CD Mus. Viva 196000-2

"10 Inventions" Song Cycle

Verses : C. P. Cavafy a. Long ago, b. Comes to rest, c.To call up the shades, d. The next table, e. Days of 1903, f. Grey, g. In the street, h. The afternoon sun, I. I' ve looked so much, j. I went.

Recording Place & Date	New York 3 Mar. 1996	Private Recording
Barytone	Timothy Sarris	UNPUBLISHED
Piano	Maria Asteriadou	

"Kassiani", for Voice and Piano

Verses : Costis Palamas.

Recording Place & Date	Westchester, N. Y. 18 May 1975	Private Recording
Soprano	Berenice Bramson	UNPUBLISHED
Piano		

"Kassiani", for Voice and Piano

Verses : Costis Palamas

Recording Place & Date	Milan 13 Nov. 1993	Private Recording
Soprano	Julia Troussa	UNPUBLISHED
Piano	Aris Garoufalis	

"Kassiani", for Voice and Piano

Verses : Costis Palamas

Recording Place & Date	New York 3 Mar. 1996	Private Recording
Soprano	Lara Nie	UNPUBLISHED
Piano	Maria Asteriadou	

"Kassiani", for Voice and Piano

Verses : Costis Palamas

Recording Place & Date	Athens 3 May 1996	Unofficial Recording
Soprano	Julia Troussa	UNPUBLISHED
Piano	Aliki Vatikioti	

"Kassiani", for Voice and Piano

Verses : Costis Palamas

Recording Place & Date	Athens 31 Oct. 1996	Radio broadcast tape
Soprano	Julia Troussa	UNPUBLISHED
Piano	Maria Asteriadou	

"Klavierstück", for Piano (1925)

Recording Place & Date	Athens 3 May 1996	Unofficial Recording
Piano	Danae Kara	UNPUBLISHED

"Klavierstück", for Piano (1925)

Recording Place & Date	Karditsa 4 Sep. 1996	Private Recording
Piano	Effie Agrafioti	UNPUBLISHED

"Klavierstück", for Piano (1925)

Recording Place & Date	Athens 4 Nov. 1996	Televised programme
Piano	Effie Agrafioti	UNPUBLISHED

"Klavierstück", for Piano (1925)

Premmiere Recording.

Recording Place & Date	Milan 1 to 4 Dec. 1996	CD Agorá AG 099.1
Piano	Danae Kara	

"Klavierstück", for Piano (1925)

Recording Place & Date	Tripolis 22 Dec. 1996	Private Recording
Piano	Effie Agrafioti	UNPUBLISHED

"The Madona of Sparti", for Voice and Piano (1916)

Verses : Angelos Sikelianos.

Recording Place & Date	Milan 13 Nov. 1993	Private Recording
Barytone	Louis Manikas	UNPUBLISHED
Piano	Aris Garoufalis	

"The Madona of Sparti", for Voice and Piano (1916)

Verses : Angelos Sikelianos.

Recording Place & Date	Athens 3 May 1996	Unofficial Recording
Barytone	Panagiotis Athanasopoulos	UNPUBLISHED
Piano	Aliki Vatikioti	

"The Madona of Sparti", for Voice and Piano (1916)

Verses : Angelos Sikelianos.

Recording Place & Date	Athens 31 Oct. 1996	Radio broadcast tape
Barytone	Louis Manikas	UNPUBLISHED
Piano	Maria Asteriadou	

"Un Morceau de Concert" in C minor for Violin & Piano (1913)

Recording Place & Date	Athens 31 Oct. 1996	Radio broadcast tape
Violin	George Demertjis	UNPUBLISHED
Piano	Maria Asteriadou	

"Mother's Heart", for Voice and Piano (1917)

Verses : Jean Richepin. Greek translation by Angelos Vlachos.

Recording Place & Date	Milan 13 Nov 1993	Private Recording
Barytone	Louis Manikas	UNPUBLISHED
Piano	Aris Garoufalis	

"Mother's Heart", for Voice and Piano (1917)

Verses : Jean Richepin. Greek translation by Angelos Vlachos.

Recording Place & Date	Athens 3 May 1996	Unofficial Recording
Soprano	Julia Troussa	UNPUBLISHED
Piano	Aliki Vatikioti	

"Mother's Heart", for Voice and Piano (1917)

Verses : Jean Richepin. Greek translation by Angelos Vlachos.

Recording Place & Date	Athens 31 Oct. 1996	Radio broadcast tape
Barytone	Louis Manikas	UNPUBLISHED
Piano	Maria Asteriadou	

"Ostinata in tre parti", for Violin & Piano (1926/27)

Allegro energico, Aria, Fuga.

Recording Place & Date	Milan 13 Nov. 1993	Private Recording
Violin	George Demertjis	UNPUBLISHED
Piano	Aris Garoufalis	

"Ostinata in tre parti", for Violin & Piano (1926/27)

Allegro energico, Aria, Fuga.

Recording Place & Date	New York 3 Mar. 1996	Private Recording
Violin	George Demertjis	UNPUBLISHED
Piano	Maria Asteriadou	

"Ostinata in tre parti", for Violin & Piano (1926/27)

Allegro energico, Aria, Fuga.

Recording Place & Date	Athens 3 May 1996	Unofficial Recording
Violin	George Demertjis	UNPUBLISHED
Piano	Danae Kara	

"Ostinata in tre parti", for Violin & Piano (1926/27)

Allegro energico, Aria, Fuga.

Recording Place & Date	Athens 31 Oct. 1996	Radio broadcast tape
Violin	George Demertjis	UNPUBLISHED
Piano	Maria Asteriadou	

"Passacaglia, Intermezzo e Fuga", for Piano (1924)

Recording Place & Date	Athens 3 May 1996	Unofficial recording
Piano	Danae Kara	UNPUBLISHED

"Passacaglia, Intermezzo e Fuga", for Piano (1924)

Recording Place & Date Karditsa 4 Sep. 1996
Piano Effie Agrafioti

Private Recording
UNPUBLISHED

"Passacaglia, Intermezzo e Fuga", for Piano (1924)

Premmiere Recording.

Recording Place & Date Milan 1 to 4 Dec. 1996
Piano Danae Kara

CD Agorá AG 099.1

"Passacaglia, Intermezzo e Fuga", for Piano (1924)

Recording Place & Date Tripolis 22 Dec. 1996
Piano Effie Agrafioti

Private Recording
UNPUBLISHED

"Rêveries au Bord de la Mer", for Piano (1924)

Premmiere Recording.

Recording Place & Date Milan 1 to 4 Dec. 1996
Piano Danae Kara

CD Agorá AG 099.1

"The sailor's death" for Voice and Piano

Verses : Ekaterini Spiliotopoulou.

Recording Place & Date Milano 13 Nov. 1993
Barytone Louis Manikas
Piano Aris Garoufalis

Private Recording
UNPUBLISHED

"The sailor's death" for Voice and Piano

Verses : Ekaterini Spiliotopoulou.

Recording Place & Date New York 3 Mar. 1996
Soprano Lara Nie
Piano Maria Asteriadou

Private Recording
UNPUBLISHED

"The sailor's death" for Voice and Piano

Verses : Ekaterini Spiliotopoulou.

Recording Place & Date	Athens 2 May 1996	Unofficial Recording
Barytone	Panagiotis Athanasopoulos	UNPUBLISHED
Piano	Aliki Vatikioti	

"The sailor's death" for Voice and Piano

Verses : Ekaterini Spiliotopoulou.

Recording Place & Date	Athens 31 Oct. 1996	Radio broadcast tape
Barytone	Louis Manikas	UNPUBLISHED
Piano	Maria Asteriadou	

"Soeur Béatrice" Miracle en 3 Acts

Premmiere Recording.

Libretto		Maurice Maeterlinck	Complete
Recording Place & Date		Pasardjik 1 to 7 Sep. 1996	CD
Orchestra		PSO	Awaiting Publication
Conductor		Byron Fidetzis	
Chorus		The Voices of Sofia	
Chorus Master		Rossitza Hristova	
Musical Preparation		Dimitris Jiakas	
Character		Interpreter	
L' Abbesse	M	Varvara Tsambali s.	
Soeur Eglantine	S	Albena Gineva	
Soeur Clémence	S	Steliana Hindalova	
Soeur Félicité	S	Nevena Scordinova	
Soeur Balbine	M	Galia Pavlova	
Soeur Régine	M	Rossitza Hristova	
Allette	M	Varvara Tsambali s.	
Béatrice-La Vierge	S	Martha Arapi	
Prince Bellidor	T	Vangelis Hadjisimos	
Le Prêtre	Bs	Mario Kiulev b.	

Libretto		Maurice Maeterlinck	Complete
Recording Place & Date		Thessaloniki 1 Nov. 1996	Radio broadcast tape
Orchestra		NBSO	UNPUBLISHED
Conductor		Byron Fidetzis	
Chorus		The Voices of Sofia	
Chorus Master		Rossitza Hristova	
Musical Preparation		Dimitris Jiakas	
Character		Interpreter	
L' Abbesse	M	Varvara Tsambali s.	
Soeur Eglantine	S	Albena Gineva	
Soeur Clémence	S	Steliana Hindalova	
Soeur Félicité	S	Nevena Scordinova	
Soeur Balbine	M	Galia Pavlova	
Soeur Régine	M	Rossitza Hristova	
Allette	M	Varvara Tsambali s.	
Béatrice-La Vierge	S	Martha Arapi	
Prince Bellidor	T	Vangelis Hadjisimos	
Le Prêtre	Bs	Mario Kiulev b.	

Sonata for Piano, in D minor, "Eine Griechische Sonate" (1920)

a. Allegro non troppo ma con passione b. Allegretto c. allegretto d. Allegro non troppo. Premmiere Recording.

Recording Place & Date	Paris Mar. 1991	CD Dante PSG 9010
Piano	Geoffrey Douglas Madge	

Sonata for Piano, in D minor, "Eine Griechische Sonate" (1920)

b. Allegretto c. allegretto d. Allegro non troppo Only the last three movements were performed.

Recording Place & Date	Athens 21 Nov. 1992	Televised Programme
Piano	Effie Agrafioti	UNPUBLISHED

Sonata for Piano, in D minor, "Eine Griechische Sonate" (1920)

a. Allegro non troppo ma con passione b. Allegretto c. allegretto d. Allegro non troppo

Recording Place & Date	Athens 26 Nov. 1996	Private recording
Piano	Alexandra Papastefanou	UNPUBLISHED

"Three Pieces for Piano" (1915-1916-1919)

1. "Béatrice" in E flat major 2. Scherzo in F minor "Sparks of Happiness" 3. Scherzo in B minor "Fête Crétoise"

Recording Place & Date	Milan 13 Nov. 1993	Private Recording
Piano	Aris Garoufalis	UNPUBLISHED

"Three Pieces for Piano" (1915-1916-1919)

1. "Béatrice" in E flat major 2. Scherzo in F minor "Sparks of Happiness" 3. Scherzo in B minor "Fête Crétoise"

Recording Place & Date	New York 3 Mar. 1996	Private Recording
Piano	Maria Asteriadou	UNPUBLISHED

"Three Pieces for Piano" (1915-1916-1919)

1. "Béatrice" in E flat major 2. Scherzo in F minor "Sparks of Happiness" 3. Scherzo in B minor "Fête Crétoise"

Recording Place & Date	Athens 3 May 1996	Unofficial Recording
Piano	Danae Kara	UNPUBLISHED

"Three Pieces for Piano", No 1 "Béatrice" in E flat major (1915)

Recording Place & Date	Karditsa 4 Sep. 1996	Private Recording
Piano	Effie Agrafioti	UNPUBLISHED

"Three Pieces for Piano", No 2, Scherzo in F minor "Sparks of Happiness" (1916)

Recording Place & Date	Karditsa 4 Sep. 1996	Private Recording
Piano	Effie Agrafioti	UNPUBLISHED

"Three Pieces for Piano", no 3 Scherzo in B minor "Fête Crétoise" (1919)

Orchestration by Nikos Skalkottas

Recording Place & Date	Athens Oct. 1996	Radio broadcast tape
Orchestra	GRSO	UNPUBLISHED
Conductor	Byron Fidetzis	

"Three Pieces for Piano", No 1 "Béatrice" in E flat major (1915)

Recording Place & Date	Athens 31 Oct. 1996	Radio broadcast tape
Piano	Maria Asteriadou	UNPUBLISHED

"Three Pieces for Piano", No 2, Scherzo in F minor "Sparks of Happiness" (1916)

Recording Place & Date	Athens 31 Oct. 1996	Private Recording
Piano	Maria Asteriadou	UNPUBLISHED

"Three Pieces for Piano", no 3 Scherzo in B minor "Fête Crétoise" (1919)

Recording Place & Date	Athens 13 Nov. 1996	Private Recording
Piano	Panos Loumakis	UNPUBLISHED

"Three Pieces for Piano" (1915-1916-1919)

1. "Béatrice" in E flat major 2. Scherzo in F minor "Sparks of Happiness" 3. Scherzo in B minor "Fête Crétoise". Premmiere Recording.

Recording Place & Date	Milan 1 to 4 Dec. 1996	CD Agorá AG 099.1
Piano	Danae Kara	

"Three Pieces for Piano", No 1 "Béatrice" in E flat major (1915)

Recording Place & Date	Tripolis 22 Dec. 1996	Private Recording
Piano	Effie Agrafioti	UNPUBLISHED

"Three Pieces for Piano", No 2 Scherzo in F minor "Sparks of Happiness" (1916)

Recording Place & Date	Tripolis 22 Dec. 1996	Private Recording
Piano	Effie Agrafioti	UNPUBLISHED

In addition to this body of original compositions, Mitropoulos transcribed Prelude and Death of Dido from Purcell's opera "Dido and Aeneas" and Beethoven's String Quartet No 14, the latter being recorded for Deutsche Grammophon in the 1970s by Leonard Bernstein and the Vienna Philharmonic Orchestra.

Eduard van Beinum
1901-1959

with valuable assistance from Malcolm Walker
and Roderick Krüsemann

Discography compiled
by John Hunt

HENDRIK ANDRIESSEN (1892-1981)

Symphony No 1

Amsterdam 15 November 1956	COA	LP: Dutch Radio 99096-99099

Miroir de peine, song cycle

Amsterdam 21 December 1952	COA Kolassi	LP: Donemus DAVS 6604

MALCOLM ARNOLD (Born 1921)

Beckus the Dandipratt, overture

London 16 December 1947	LPO	78: Decca K 1844

JOHANN CHRISTIAN BACH (1735-1782)

Sinfonia in B flat

Amsterdam 6-7 October 1958	COA	45: Philips A400 127E LP: Philips G05378R/6768 023 LP: Epic LC 3749/BC 1112

Sinfonia in D

Amsterdam 6-7 October 1958	COA	45: Philips A400 128E LP: Philips G05378R/6768 023 LP: Epic LC 3749/BC 1112

JOHANN SEBASTIAN BACH (1685-1750)

Suite No 1

Amsterdam 31 May-2 June 1955	COA	LP: Philips ABL 3136/A00350L LP: Epic LC 3194

Suite No 2

Amsterdam 31 May-2 June 1955	COA Barwahser	LP: Philips ABL 3136/A00350L LP: Epic LC 3194 CD: Philips 420 8572

Suite No 2, Polonaise and badinerie

Amsterdam 23 September 1949	COA Barwahser	78: Decca X 10261 78: Philips (Belgium) A 1099

Suite No 3

Amsterdam 23 September 1949	COA	78: Decca X 10259-10261 78: Philips (Belgium) A 1097-1099
Amsterdam 3 April 1956	COA	LP: Philips ABL 3137/A00351L/G05322R LP: Epic LC 3332

Suite No 4

Amsterdam 10 April 1956	COA	LP: Philips ABL 3137/A00350L LP: Epic LC 3332

Piano Concerto in D minor

Amsterdam 2 October 1947	COA Lipatti	LP: Discocorp MLG 80 LP: Jecklin 541 LP: Turnabout THS 65111 CD: Jecklin JD 5412

Concertgebouw, Amsterdam
donderdag 9 januari 1936 te 8.15

abonnementsconcert

Serie A en B

het concertgebouw-orkest

onder leiding van

Eduard van Beinum

Johannes Brahms
1833—1897

Variaties over een thema van Jos. Haydn (op. 56a)

P. I. Tschaikowsky
1840—1893

Concert (op. 35)
voor viool en orkest

Allegro
Canzonetta
Finale: Allegro vivacissimo

solist: Bronislaw Huberman

Pauze

Igor Strawinsky
geb. 1882

Le Sacre du Printemps
Tableaux de la Russie Païenne en deux parties

Concertgebouw, Amsterdam
donderdag 23 januari 1936 te 8.15

abonnementsconcert

Serie A en B

het concertgebouw-orkest
onder leiding van

Eduard van Beinum

F. Mendelssohn-Bartholdy
1809—1847

Ouverture voor Shakespeare's
„A midsummernight's-dream"

Luigi Boccherini
1743—1805

Concerto No. III (G gr. t.)
per il violoncello obligato con due violini, alto, viola e basso

Allegro non troppo
Adagio
Allegro

solist: Marix Loevensohn

Pauze

Anton Bruckner
1824—1896

Zevende symphonie

Allegro moderato
Adagio
Scherzo
Finale

De Clavecin Pleyel is uit het magazijn van de firma Duwaer & Naessens, Stadhouderskade 19-20

HENK BADINGS (1907-1987)

Concerto for 2 violins and orchestra

Date not confirmed	COA Krebbers, Olof	Unpublished radio broadcast

BELA BARTOK (1881-1945)

Concerto for orchestra

Amsterdam 20 September 1948	COA	78: Decca AK 2042-2046 78: Decca (USA) EDA 105 78: London LA 91 LP: Decca LXT 2529 LP: London LLP 5 Some commentators described this as the work's premiere recording, but it was first recorded in 1946 by Reiner and the Pittsburgh SO

Music for strings, percussion and celesta

Amsterdam 13-14 October 1955	COA	LP: Philips ABL 3163/A 00353L/6768 023 LP: Epic LC 3274

LUDWIG VAN BEETHOVEN (1770-1827)

Symphony No 2

Amsterdam 22 May 1954	COA	LP: Philips ABR 4036/A 00720R/GBL 5575

Piano Concerto No 1

Amsterdam 1-2 March 1959	COA Casadesus	LP: Philips ABL 3299/L 09423L/ A 01424L/835 526AY LP: Columbia (USA) ML 5437/MS 6111 3216 0056 LP: CBS 72200

Piano Concerto No 4

Amsterdam 1-2 March 1959	COA Casadesus	LP: Philips ABL 3299/L 09423L/ A 01424L/835 526AY LP: Columbia (USA) ML 5437/MS 6111 3216 0056 LP: CBS 72200/10002

Violin Concerto

Amsterdam 4 June 1957	COA Grumiaux	LP: Philips L 00434L/ZKY 894 048

Coriolan, overture

London 25 February- 19 March 1952	LPO	LP: Decca LW 5015/ACL 97 LP: London LLP 357/LD 9021/B 19026

Egmont, overture

Amsterdam 23 September 1949	COA	78: Decca X 10258
London 25 February- 19 March 1952	LPO	LP: Decca LW 5015/ACL 97/ECM 556/ECS 556 LP: London LLP 357/LD 9021/B 19026

Fidelio, overture

London 25 February- 19 March 1952	LPO	LP: Decca LW 5018/ACL 97 LP: London LLP 357/LD 9024/B 19026

Die Geschöpfe des Prometheus, incidental music

London 25 February- 19 March 1952	LPO	LP: Decca LXT 2741 LP: London LLP 577 <u>Overture only</u> LP: Decca LW 5018/ACL 97/ECM 556/ECS 556 LP: London LD 9024

Leonore No 1, overture

London 2 May 1949	LPO	78: Decca K 28151/X 311 78: London T 5162 LP: London LLP 49

Leonore No 2, overture

Walthamstow 9 March 1946	COA	78: Decca AK 1431-1432/X 10028-10029 78: Decca (USA) ED 4

Leonore No 3, overture

London 25 February- 19 March 1952	LPO	LP: Decca LW 5016/ACL 97/ECM 556/ECS 556 LP: London LLP 357/LD 9022/B 19026

Die Weihe des Hauses, overture

London 11 April 1950	LPO	LP: Decca LW 5016/ACL 97 LP: London LLP 357/LD 9022/B 19026

HECTOR BERLIOZ (1803-1869)

Symphonie fantastique

Amsterdam 24-26 November 1941	COA	78: Telefunken SK 3248-3253
Amsterdam 20-23 September 1943	COA	Polydor unpublished
Amsterdam 9 September 1946	COA	78: Decca K 1626-1631/AK 1626-1631/ X 10246-10251 78: Decca (USA) EDA 56 78: London LA 111 LP: London LLP 35
Amsterdam 10 September 1951	COA	LP: Decca LXT 2642/ACL 27/ECM 561/ECS 561 LP: London LLP 489/B 19010 CD: Beulah 1PD 17 Also issued on LP on London's Richmond label

Benvenuto Cellini, overture

Amsterdam 20 September 1949	COA	78: Decca X 10255-10256 78: Philips (Belgium) A 1112-1113

Le carnaval romain, overture

Amsterdam September 1951	COA	LP: Decca LW 5176/ECM 561/ECS 561 Also issued on LP on London's Richmond label
Amsterdam 24-25 September 1956	COA	45: Philips S313 048F LP: Philips 6768 023

La damnation de Faust, Marche hongroise

Walthamstow 9 March 1946	COA	78: Decca K 1648 78: Polydor 68327 CD: Beulah 1PD 17
Amsterdam September 1951	COA	45: Decca 45-71117 LP: Decca LX 3096 LP: London LL 1520/LS 620

La damnation de Faust, Menuet des follets

Walthamstow 9 March 1946	COA	78: Decca K 1648 78: Polydor 68327 CD: Beulah 1PD 17
Amsterdam September 1951	COA	45: Decca 45-71117 LP: Decca LW 5176/LX 3096 LP: London LL 1520/LS 620

La damnation de Faust, Ballet des sylphes

Walthamstow 9 March 1946	COA	78: Decca K 1649 CD: Beulah 1PD 17
Amsterdam September 1951	COA	LP: Decca LW 5176/LX 3096 LP: London LL 1520/LS 620

Les troyens, Marche troyenne

Amsterdam 18 March 1946	COA	78: Decca K 1649 CD: Beulah 1PD 17

COMMODORE CINEMA, HAMMERSMITH

Sunday, January 9th, 1949 at 3 p.m.

LONDON PHILHARMONIC ORCHESTRA

(Leader: DAVID WISE)

MENDELSSOHN: Overture, Fingal's Cave
BEETHOVEN: Piano Concerto No. 5 in E flat (Emperor)
ELGAR: Wand of Youth, Suite No. I
TCHAIKOVSKY: Overture-Fantasia, Romeo and Juliet

Solo Pianoforte: **POUISHNOFF**

Conductor: **EDUARD VAN BEINUM**

All seats bookable: Circle 5/6, 4/6
Stalls 4/6, 3/6, 2/6

From: The Commodore Cinema, Hammersmith (Tel. RIV 2896)

ROYAL ALBERT HALL

Eduard van Beinum

will conduct a **BEETHOVEN CYCLE** with the

LONDON PHILHARMONIC ORCHESTRA

Thursdays at 7.30 p.m.

January 27th, 1949

Overture, Leonora No. 3
Symphony No. 1 in C major
Symphony No. 3 in E flat (Eroica)

February 3rd, 1949

Overture, Leonora No. 2
Violin Concerto in D
Symphony No. 2 in D

Solo Violin:
GIOCONDA DE VITO

February 10th, 1949

Overture, Leonora No. 1
Rondino for Wind Instruments
Symphony No. 4 in B flat
Symphony No. 5 in C minor

February 17th 1949

Overture, Egmont
Symphony No. 6 in F (Pastoral)
Symphony No. 7 in A

February 24th, 1949

Symphony No. 8 in F
Symphony No. 9 in D minor (Choral)

Soprano: **MAIDI ARNOLD** Contralto: **NANCY EVANS**
Tenor: **PARRY JONES** Bass: **WILLIAM PARSONS**

LONDON PHILHARMONIC CHOIR

(Chorus Master: FREDERIC JACKSON)

TICKETS: Subscription (5 concerts) booking opens Dec. 6: 53/9 45/- 33/9 27/1 17/11 13 4
Single concert, booking opens Jan. 20 1949: 12/- 10/- 7/6 6/- 4/- 3/- 2/- (standing)
from Box Office (KEN 8212), Chappell's 50 New Bond Street (MAY 7600) and agents

GEORGES BIZET (1838-1875)

L'Arlésienne, suite no 1

Amsterdam 20-23 September 1943	COA	78: Polydor 68183-68184/69184-69185
London 11 February 1950	LPO	78: Decca AK 2385-2386 LP: Decca LXT 2510/ACL 9 LP: London LLP 179/B 19013

L'Arlésienne, minuet and farandole from suite no 2

Amsterdam 20-23 September 1943	COA	78: Polydor 68185/69186
London 11 February 1950	LPO	78: Decca AK 2387 LP: Decca LXT 2510/ACL 9 LP: London LLP 179/B 19013

ALEXANDER BORODIN (1833-1887)

Polovtsian Dances

London 11 April 1950	LPO LPO Choir	78: Decca AX 531-532 LP: Decca LXT 2518 LP: London LLP 203/B 19032

JOHANNES BRAHMS (1833-1897)

Symphony No 1

Amsterdam 20 September 1947	COA	78: Decca K 1895-1899/AK 1895-1899/ X 10121-10125
Amsterdam 17 September 1951	COA	LP: Decca LXT 2675/LXT 5366/ACL 71/ ECM 793/ECS 793 LP: London LL 490/B 19016 LP: Telefunken (USA) K4R 1
Amsterdam 6-7 October 1958	COA	LP: Philips ABL 3283/A 00504L/ SABL 124/835 015AY/ZKY 894.036 CD: Philips 420 8542

Symphony No 2

Amsterdam 17-19 May 1954	COA	LP: Philips ABL 3020/A 00218L/GBL 5596

Symphony No 3

London 2-23 March 1946	LPO	78: Decca K 1448-1452/AK 1448-1452 78: Decca (USA) EDA 22
Amsterdam 24-25 September 1956	COA	LP: Philips GBL 5524/S 06150R

Symphony No 4

Amsterdam 1-3 May 1958	COA	LP: Philips ABL 3310/A 00502L/ SABL 100/835 000AY/ZKY 894 003

Piano Concerto No 1

Amsterdam May 1953	COA Curzon	LP: Decca LXT 2825/ACL 277 LP: London LLP 850 CD: Decca 421 1432

Violin Concerto

Amsterdam 3-4 July 1958	COA Grumiaux	LP: Philips L 09007L/L 02356L/ SAL 3526/610 105VR/835 008AY/ 835 234LY

Haydn Variations

Amsterdam 24-26 November 1941	COA	78: Telefunken SK 3746-3747
London 2 May 1949	LPO	78: Decca X 299-300/AX 299-300 78: Decca (USA) LA 116
Amsterdam December 1952	COA	LP: Decca LXT 2778/LW 5269/ACL 44/ ECM 520/ECS 520 LP: London LLP 735/B 19024 CD: Decca 421 1432
Amsterdam 25 September 1958	COA	LP: Philips GBL 5524/835 013AY CD: Philips 420 8542

Alto Rhapsody

Amsterdam 24 February 1958	COA Heynis	45: Philips A400 057E LP: Philips GL 5686/L 09007L/G 05319R G 03163L CD: Philips 420 8542

Academic Festial Overture

Amsterdam November 1952	COA	LP: Decca LXT 2778/LW 5041/ACL 44/ ECM 520/ECS 520 LP: London LLP 735/B 19024
Amsterdam 26-27 September 1958	COA	LP: Philips 835 013AY

Tragic Overture

Amsterdam November 1952	COA	LP: Decca LXT 2778/LW 5041/ACL 44/ ECM 520/ECS 520 LP: London LLP 735/B 19024
Amsterdam 26-27 September 1958	COA	LP: Philips 835 013AY

BIZET
SUITE FROM
CARMEN
ANTHONY COLLINS
conducting
THE
LONDON PHILHARMONIC
ORCHESTRA
SUITE FROM
L'ARLÉSIENNE
EDUARD VAN BEINUM
conducting
THE
LONDON PHILHARMONIC
ORCHESTRA
LONG
33⅓
RPM
PLAYING
DECCA
ffrr
FLEXIBLE
Long playing microgroove full frequency range recording
LXT 2510

SCHUBERT
MENDELSSOHN
ROSAMUNDE
A MIDSUMMER NIGHT'S DREAM
INCIDENTAL MUSIC
OPUS 26
INCIDENTAL MUSIC
EDUARD VAN BEINUM
conducting
THE CONCERTGEBOUW ORCHESTRA OF AMSTERDAM
LONG PLAYING
RPM
DECCA
FLEXIBLE
Long playing microgroove full frequency range recording
LXT 2770

ffrr

BENJAMIN BRITTEN (1913-1976)

Spring Symphony

Amsterdam 9 July 1949	COA Choirs Vincent, Ferrier, Pears	CD: Decca 440 0632 World premiere performance

Young Person's Guide to the orchestra

Amsterdam 16 September 1953	COA	LP: Decca LXT 2886/ACL 30/ECM 712/ECS 712 LP: London LLP 917/B 19040 CD: Decca 440 0632

Peter Grimes, 4 Sea interludes

Amsterdam 15 September 1947	COA	78: Decca K 1702-1704 78: Decca (USA) EDA 50 78: London LA 201
Amsterdam 14 September 1953	COA	LP: Decca LXT 2886/LW 5244/ACL 162/ ECM 712/ECS 712 LP: London LLP 917 CD: Decca 440 0632

Peter Grimes, Passacaglia

Amsterdam 15 September 1947	COA	78: Decca K 1704 78: Decca (USA) EDA 50 78: London LA 201
Amsterdam 15 September 1953	COA	LP: Decca LXT 2886/ACL 162/ECM 712/ECS 712 LP: London LLP 917

ANTON BRUCKNER (1824-1896)

Symphony No 5

Amsterdam 12 March 1959	COA	LP: Philips 6768 023 CD: Philips 456 2492

Symphony No 7

Amsterdam 10 September 1947	COA	78: Decca K 1916-1923/AK 1916-1923 78: London LA 94
Amsterdam May 1953	COA	LP: Decca LXT 2829-2830/ECM 571/ECS 571 CD: Decca 421 1392

Symphony No 8

Amsterdam 6-9 June 1955	COA	LP: Philips ABL 3086-3087/ A 00294-00295L LP: Epic SC 6011 CD: Philips 442 7302

Symphony No 9

Amsterdam 17-19 September 1956	COA	LP: Philips A 00390L/ZKY 894 050 CD: Philips 442 7312

Symphony No 9, Adagio only

Amsterdam 4 October 1956	COA	LP: Dutch Radio 99096-99099

LUIGI CHERUBINI (1760-1842)

Anacreon, overture

Amsterdam 21 September 1949	COA	Decca unpublished

JEREMIAH CLARKE (1674-1707)

Trumpet Voluntary, arranged by Wood

Amsterdam 19 May 1952	COA	LP: Decca LX 3096/ECM 771/ECS 771 LP: London LS 620

LEX VAN DELDEN (1919-1988)

Harp Concerto

Amsterdam 20 September 1952	COA Berghout	CD: Etcetera KTC 2024

CLAUDE DEBUSSY (1862-1918)

La mer

Amsterdam 27-28 May 1957	COA	LP: Philips A 00441L/835 001AY/ 6816 102/ZKY 894 005

Nocturnes

Amsterdam 27-28 May 1957	COA Collegium Choir	LP: Philips A 00441L/835 001AY/ZKY894 005 6768 023

Images pour orchestre

Amsterdam 24-25 May 1954	COA	LP: Philips ABR 4032/A 00722R/6768 023

Berceuse héroique

Amsterdam 27-28 May 1957	COA	LP: Philips A 00441L/835 003AY/ 835 009AY/6768 023 CD: Philips 438 7422

Printemps

Amsterdam 15 December 1956	COA	LP: Dutch Radio 99096-99099

Marche écossaise

Amsterdam 27-28 May 1957	COA	LP: Philips A 00441L/835 003AY/ 835 009AY/6768 023

Danse sacrée et danse profane

Amsterdam May 1952	Amsterdam Chamber Music Society Berghout	LP: Decca LX 3097 LP: London LS 621/LL 1552 CD: Etcetera KTC 2024

Concertgebouw
Donderdag 13 Februari 1941 te 7.15 uur

Abonnementsconcert

serie A en B
dirigent: Eduard van Beinum

Henry Purcell
1659?—1695

Pavane en Chaconne
voor strijkorkest

L. van Beethoven
1770—1827

Vijfde concert Es gr. t., op. 73
voor piano en orkest

Allegro
Adagio un poco mosso
Rondo: Allegro

soliste: Elly Ney

Pauze

P. I. Tschaikowsky
1840—1893

Vierde symphonie f kl. t., op. 36
Andante sostenuto — Moderato con anima
Andantino in modo di canzona
Scherzo: Pizzicato ostinato
Finale: Allegro con fuoco

ROYAL ALBERT HALL

THURSDAY SYMPHONY CONCERTS

Thursday, November 27th at 7.30

LONDON PHILHARMONIC ORCHESTRA

TCHAIKOVSKY : Overture-Fantasia: Romeo and Juliet

WAGNER: Siegfried Idyll

BERLIOZ: Three Pieces from "The Damnation of Faust"
(a) Minuet of the Will o' the Wisps
(b) Dance of the Sylphs
(c) Hungarian March

FRANCK: Symphony in D minor

Conductor:

EDUARD VAN BEINUM

TICKETS: **15/-, 12/6, 10/6, 7/6, 5/-, 3/6, 2/6**

from Box Office (KEN 8212) and usual agents

ALPHONS DIEPENBROCK (1862-1921)

Marsyas, Prelude and entr'acte

Amsterdam May 1953	COA	LP: Decca LXT 2873

Te deum

Amsterdam 6 December 1956	COA Toonkunst Choir Spoorenberg, Merriman, Haefliger, Bogtman	LP: Philips S 04032L CD: Donemus CVCD 7/BFO-A3 Recorded at the concert marking Van Beinum's 25 years as conductor of Concertgebouw Orchestra

ANTONIN DVORAK (1841-1904)

Slavonic Dance no 3

Amsterdam 16 September 1949	COA	78: Decca X 10254/AX 355

Slavonic Dance no 5

Amsterdam 20-23 September 1943	COA	78: Polydor 68238

Slavonic Dance no 8

Amsterdam 20-23 September 1943	COA	78: Polydor 68238

EDWARD ELGAR (1857-1934)

Cello Concerto

London 14 May 1949- 12 April 1950	LPO Pini	LP: Decca LXT 5279/LX 3023/ECM 565/ECS 565 LP: London LPS 95 CD: Beulah 2PD 15

Cockaigne, overture

London 13 May 1949	LPO	78: Decca AX 296-297 78: London LA 96 LP: Decca LXT 5279/LXT 2525/ ECM 564/ECS 564 LP: London LLP 43 CD: Beulah 2PD 15

Elegy for strings

London 13 May 1949	LPO	78: Decca AK 2190 CD: Beulah 2PD 15

Wand of Youth, suite no 1

London 4-5 February 1949	LPO	78: Decca AK 2190-2192 LP: Decca LXT 2525/LXT 5279/ACL 224 LP: London LLP 43 CD: Beulah 2PD 15

Wand of Youth, suite no 2

London 13 February 1950	LPO	78: Decca AX 465-466 LP: Decca ECM 564/ECS 564 CD: Beulah 2PD 15

RUDOLF ESCHER (1912-1980)

Musique pour l'esprit en deuil

Amsterdam 1 September 1954	COA	LP: Donemus DAVS 6403

MARIUS FLOTHUIS (Born 1914)

Symfonische muziek

Amsterdam 19 June 1958	COA	LP: Donemus DAVS 6101

CESAR FRANCK (1822-1890)

Variations symphoniques pour piano et orchestre

Amsterdam 17-21 May 1943	COA Anda	78: Polydor 68132-68133/69099-69100 LP: Decca (USA) DL 9542

Psyché, symphonic poem

Amsterdam September 1951	COA	LP: Decca LXT 2829/LW 5069 LP: London LL 1520 CD: Decca 421 1402

Psyché et Eros (Psyché)

Amsterdam 21 September 1947	COA	78: Decca X 10189

CHRISTOPH WILLIBALD GLUCK (1714-1787)

Alceste, overture

Amsterdam 21 September 1949	COA	78: Decca X 10190

Iphigenie in Aulis overture may also have been recorded at this session

EDVARD GRIEG (1843-1907)

Elegiac melodies

Amsterdam 1-3 May 1958	COA	45: Philips S313 043F LP: Philips 835 003AY/6768 023

GEORGE FRIDERIC HANDEL (1685-1759)

Music for the Royal fireworks, suite arranged by Harty

Amsterdam 19 May 1952	COA	LP: Decca LXT 2792/LXT 5379/LX 3096/ ACL 162/ECM 771/ECS 771 LP: London LS 620/LLP 760

Water music

Amsterdam 1-5 July 1958	COA	LP: Philips ABL 3249/A 00491L/SABL 125/ 835 004AY/ZKY 894 007/6540 068 LP: Epic LC 3551/LC 3749/BC 1016/BC 1112 CD: Philips 420 8572 Excerpts 45: Philips A400 119E

Water music, suite arranged by Harty

London 5 May 1950	LPO	78: Decca AX 495-496 LP: Decca LXT 2534/LXT 2792/LXT 5379/ LW 5263/ACL 162/ECM 771/ECS 771 LP: London LLP 214/LLP 760/B 19101

FRANZ JOSEF HAYDN (1732-1809)

Symphony No 94 "Surprise"

Amsterdam 24 September 1951	COA	LP: Decca LXT 2686/LW 5264/ACL 41 LP: London LL 491

Symphony No 96 "Miracle"

Amsterdam 21 September 1947	COA	78: Decca K 1855-1857/X 10208-10210
Amsterdam December 1952	COA	LP: Decca LXT 2847/ACL 196 LP: London LLP 854

Symphony No 97

Amsterdam December 1952	COA	LP: Decca LXT 2847/ACL 196 LP: London LLP 854

Symphony No 100 "Military"

London 29 November 1946	LPO	78: Decca AK 1808-1810 78: London LA 143 LP: Decca LXT 2683/ACL 41 LP: London LLP 339

Symphony No 101 "Clock"

Amsterdam 4 March 1959	COA	LP: Pastmasters PM 37

HANS HENKEMANS (Born 1913)

Violin Concerto

Amsterdam 20-21 May 1954	COA Olof	LP: Philips A 00219L CD: Donemus CVCD 7/BFO-A3

ZOLTAN KODALY (1882-1967)

Hary Janos suite

Amsterdam 11-12 April 1956	COA	LP: Philips ABL 3163/A 00353L/6768 023

HANS KOX (Born 1930)

Concerto for horn, trumpet and trombone

Amsterdam 7 October 1956	COA Bos, Komst, Maassen	LP: Dutch Radio 99096-99099

EDOUARD LALO (1823-1892)

Symphonie espagnole pour violon et orchestre

London 3-4 March 1953	LPO Campoli	LP: Decca LXT 2801 LP: London LLP 763

Concertgebouw
Donderdag 6 Januari 1938 te 8.15

Abonnementsconcert

serie A en B
dirigent: Eduard van Beinum

L. van Beethoven
1770—1827

Ouverture „Leonore" No. 1

Derde concert (c kl. t., op. 37)
voor piano en orkest
Allegro con brio
Largo
Rondo: Allegro
solist: Egon Petri

Pauze

Anton Bruckner
1824—1896

Zevende symphonie (E gr. t.)
Allegro moderato
Adagio
Scherzo
Finale

Concertgebouw
Donderdag 12 Januari 1939 te 8.15

Abonnementsconcert

serie A en B
dirigent: Eduard van Beinum

Joseph Haydn
1732—1809

* Symphonie no. 99, Es gr. t.
Adagio — Vivace assai
Adagio
Menuetto: Allegretto
Vivace

Leoš Janáček
1854—1928

Sinfonietta

Pauze

L. van Beethoven
1770—1827

Vierde concert G gr. t., op. 58
voor piano en orkest
Allegro moderato
Andante con moto
Rondo: Vivace

solist: Artur Schnabel

* *eerste uitvoering*

BERTUS VAN LIER (1906-1972)

Divertimento facile

Amsterdam 15 October 1958	COA	LP: Donemus DAVS 6601

GUSTAV MAHLER (1860-1911)

Symphony No 4

Amsterdam April- May 1952	COA Ritchie	LP: Decca LXT 2718/ACL 212/ECM 618/ECS 618 LP: London LL 618 LP: Vox VSPS 16 CD: Decca 421 1402

Das Lied von der Erde

Amsterdam 3-6 December 1956	COA Merriman, Haefliger	LP: Philips A 00410-00411L/GL 5798/ ZKY 894 120/6780 013 CD: Philips awaiting publication

Lieder eines fahrenden Gesellen

London 27 November 1946	LPO Zareska	78: Decca AK 1624-1625 78: London LA 224
Amsterdam 8-12 December 1956	COA Merriman	LP: Philips A 00410-00411L/6780 013

FELIX MENDELSSOHN-BARTHOLDY (1809-1847)

Symphony No 4 "Italian"

Amsterdam 2-4 June 1955	COA	LP: Philips SBR 6202/S 06073R/GBL 5578/ 6768 023

Violin Concerto

London 1 May 1949	LPO Campoli	78: Decca AX 290-292 78: London LA 98 LP: Decca LXT 2904/LX 3001/ACL 4 LP: London LPS 90/B 19021

Hebrides, overture

London 4-5 February 1949	LPO	78: Decca K 2237

A Midsummer Night's Dream, overture

Amsterdam May 1952	COA	LP: Decca LXT 2770/LW 5046/ LW 5295/ACL 85 LP: London LLP 622/B 19035

A Midsummer Night's Dream, intermezzo

Amsterdam 12 September 1946	COA	78: Decca K 1768 78: London LA 179

A Midsummer Night's Dream, nocturne

Amsterdam 12 September 1946	COA	78: Decca K 1768 78: London LA 179
Amsterdam May 1952	COA	LP: Decca LXT 2770/LW 5295/ACL 85 LP: London LLP 622/B 19035

A Midsummer Night's Dream, scherzo

Amsterdam 12 September 1946	COA	78: Decca K 1769 78: London LA 179
Amsterdam May 1952	COA	LP: Decca LXT 2770/LW 5295/ACL 85 LP: London LLP 622/B 19035

WOLFGANG AMADEUS MOZART (1756-1791)

Symphony No 29

Amsterdam 25 May 1956	COA	LP: Philips A 00398L/6768 023 LP: Epic LC 3354

Symphony No 33

Amsterdam 24 September 1951	COA	78: Decca K 23278-23280 LP: Decca LXT 2686/LW 5315/ACL 107 LP: London LLP 491

Symphony No 35 "Haffner"

London 1 May 1952	LPO	78: Decca AX 467-468 LP: Decca LXT 2534/LW 5262/ACL 66 LP: London LLP 214

Piano Concerto No 9

Amsterdam 1950	COA Hess	CD: Pearl GEMMCD 9114 This performance could not be confirmed in the Concertgebouw's archives

Piano Concerto No 24

Amsterdam 21 September 1948	COA Long	78: Decca AK 2075-2078 78: London LA 134 LP: Decca ACL 168 LP: London LLP 29

Clarinet Concerto

Amsterdam 29 May 1957	COA De Wilde	LP: Philips ABL 3217/A 00440L/ ZKY 894 018 LP: Epic LC 3456

Flute and Harp Concerto

Amsterdam 6 June 1957	COA Barwahser Berghout	LP: Philips ABL 3217/A 00440L/ ZKY 894 018 LP: Epic LC 3456 CD: Etcetera KTC 2024

Serenade No 9 "Posthorn"

Amsterdam 22-23 May 1956	COA	LP: Philips A 00398L LP: Epic LC 3354

Così fan tutte, overture

London 1 May 1950	LPO	Decca unpublished

OTTO NICOLAI (1810-1849)

Die lustigen Weiber von Windsor, overture

Amsterdam 10 April 1956	COA	45: Philips NBE 11043/N402 063E LP: Philips GL 5686/G03163L/6768 023

WILLEM PIJPER (1894-1947)

Symphony No 3 with piano obbligato

Amsterdam May 1953	COA Curzon	LP: Decca LXT 2873

Piano Concerto

Amsterdam 28 May 1954	COA Henkemans	LP: Philips A 00219L

Zes sinfonische epigrammen

Amsterdam 29 May 1954	COA	LP: Philips A 00219L

MAURICE RAVEL (1875-1937)

Bolero

Amsterdam 30 June 1958	COA	LP: Philips G 05349R/835 009AY/ ZKY 894 011/6530 017

Introduction and allegro for harp and chamber ensemble

Amsterdam December 1952	Amsterdam Chamber Music Society Berghout	LP: Decca LX 3097 LP: London LS 621/LL 1552 CD: Etcetera KTC 2024

Rapsodie espagnole

Amsterdam 10 September 1946	COA	78: Decca AK 2093-2094
Amsterdam 7 October 1956	COA	LP: Dutch Radio 99096-99099

La valse

Amsterdam 25 September 1958	COA	LP: Philips G 05349R/835 009AY/ 6530 017

MAX REGER (1873-1916)

Variations and Fugue on a theme of Mozart

Amsterdam 17-21 May 1943	COA	78: Polydor 68222-68226/69192-69196 78: Decca (USA) DGS 2 LP: Decca (USA) DL 9565

Ballet suite

Amsterdam 17-21 May 1943	COA	78: Polydor 68227-68229/69424-69426 78: Decca (USA) DGS 18

NIKOLAI RIMSKY-KORSAKOV (1844-1908)

Scheherazade

Amsterdam 17 July 1956	COA	LP: Philips A 00373L/S 60131R G05407R/6768 023

A performance of Scheherazade by van Beinum and the Concertgebouw Orchestra appeared on LP Movimento musica 01.044: it is not known whether this is the commercial recording or a live performance

WOENSDAG 28 EN DONDERDAG 29 NOVEMBER 1951 - 8.15 UUR

ABONNEMENTSCONCERT - SERIE B No. 6

HET CONCERTGEBOUWORKEST

Dirigent **Eduard van Beinum**
Solist **Stefan Askenase**, piano

ALBERT ROUSSEL
1869-1937

Sinfonietta
VOOR STRIJKORKEST

Allegro molto
Andante
Allegro

ROBERT SCHUMANN
1810-1856

Concert a kl. t., op. 54
VOOR PIANO EN ORKEST

Allegro - Andante espressivo - Tempo primo - Allegro molto
Intermezzo: Andantino grazioso
Allegro vivace

N. RIMSKY-KORSAKOFF
1844-1908

Sheherazade, op. 35
SYMPHONISCHE SUITE NAAR „DUIZEND EN ÉÉN NACHT"

De zee en het schip van Sindbad
Het verhaal van prins Kalender
De jonge Prins en de jonge Prinses
Feest in Bagdad - De zee - Het schip slaat te pletter tegen een rots - Besluit

STEINWAY & SONS' CONCERTVLEUGEL

CONCERTGEBOUW - AMSTERDAM

WOENSDAG 19 MAART / DONDERDAG 20 MAART 1958 - 8.15 UUR

ABONNEMENTSCONCERT - SERIE B Nr. 16

HET CONCERTGEBOUWORKEST

Dirigent **Eduard van Beinum**
Solist **Zino Francescatti,** viool

L. VAN BEETHOVEN
1770-1827

Ouverture „Leonore", nr. 1, op. 138 (1805)

Concert, D gr. t., op. 61 (1806)

VOOR VIOOL EN ORKEST

Allegro ma non troppo
Larghetto
Rondo: Allegro

Cadenzen van Fritz Kreisler

BÉLA BARTÓK
1881-1945

Concert voor orkest (1943)

Introduzione: Andante non troppo - allegro vivace
Giuoco delle coppie: Allegretto scherzando
Elegia: Andante, non troppo
Intermezzo interrotto: Allegretto
Finale: Pesante - Presto

GIOACHINO ROSSINI (1792-1868)

Guillaume Tell, overture

Amsterdam May 1952	COA	LP: Decca LXT 2773/LW 5039/ACL 15 LP: London LL 358/LD 9032/B 19004

La gazza ladra, overture

Amsterdam May 1952	COA	LP: Decca LXT 2773/LW 5017/ACL 15 LP: London LLP 358/LD 9023/B 19004

La scala di seta, overture

Amsterdam May 1952	COA	LP: Decca LXT 2773/LW 5017/ACL 15 LP: London LLP 358/LD 9023/B 19004

Semiramide, overture

Amsterdam May 1952	COA	LP: Decca LXT 2773/LW 5039/ACL 15 LP: London LLP 358/LD 9032/B 19004

FRANZ SCHUBERT (1797-1828)

Symphony No 3

Amsterdam 6-9 June 1955	COA	LP: Philips ABL 3086/A 00294L LP: Epic SC 6011

Symphony No 4 "Tragic"

Amsterdam December 1952	COA	LP: Decca LXT 2779/ACL 152/LW 50103 LP: London LLP 736

Symphony No 5

Amsterdam 17 September 1946	COA	78: Decca AX 451-453 LP: Decca LX 3082/ACL 152 LP: London LS 253

Symphony No 6

Amsterdam 22-25 May 1957	COA	LP: Philips A 09002L/422 1771/6768 023 CD: Philips 422 1772

Symphony No 8 "Unfinished"

Amsterdam 22-25 May 1957	COA	LP: Philips A 09002L/G 05304R 6768 023

Rosamunde, overture

Amsterdam May 1952	COA	LP: Decca LXT 2770/LW 5046/ACL 85 LP: London LLP 622/B 19035

Rosamunde, entr'acte no 3

Amsterdam May 1952	COA	LP: Decca LXT 2770/ACL 85 LP: London LLP 622/B 19035

Rosamunde, ballet music no 2

Amsterdam May 1952	COA	LP: Decca LXT 2770/ACL 85 LP: London LLP 622/B 19035

JEAN SIBELIUS (1865-1957)

Violin Concerto

London 4-5 March 1953	LPO Damen	LP: Decca LXT 2813

En saga

Amsterdam December 1952	COA	LP: Decca LXT 2776/ACL 76/ECM 655/ECS 655 LP: London LLP 737

Finlandia

Amsterdam 23 September 1949	COA	78: Decca X 10266
Amsterdam 7-8 June 1957	COA	45: Philips A400 034E LP: Philips 835 003AY/6747 204/6768 023 LP: Readers Digest RD 6997/RDS 6997

The Swan of Tuonela

Amsterdam 24-26 November 1941	COA	78: Telefunken SK 3236 78: Ultraphon G 18115

Tapiola

Amsterdam December 1952	COA	LP: Decca LXT 2776/ACL 76/ECM 655/ECS 655 LP: London LLP 737

Valse triste

Amsterdam 7-8 June 1957	COA	45: Philips A400 034E LP: Philips 835 003AY/SABL 103/6768 023

BEDRICH SMETANA (1824-1884)

The Moldau (Ma Vlast)

Amsterdam 20-23 September 1943	COA	Polydor unpublished
Amsterdam 15 September 1949	COA	78: Decca 10253-10254/AX 354-355

JOHN PHILIP SOUSA (1854-1932)

Stars and stripes forever, march

Amsterdam 27 September 1958	COA	45: Philips ABE 10245/SABE 2010/ SBF 182/S313 122F LP: Philips GL 5680/G03160L/ 6718 010/6768 023

RICHARD STRAUSS (1864-1949)

Don Juan

Amsterdam 23 September 1949	COA	78: Decca X 10262-10263

CONCERTGEBOUW - AMSTERDAM

WOENSDAG 14 NOVEMBER / DONDERDAG 15 NOVEMBER 1956 / 8.15 UUR

ABONNEMENTSCONCERT - SERIE B Nr. 6

HET CONCERTGEBOUWORKEST

Dirigent **Eduard van Beinum**
Soliste **Dame Myra Hess**, piano

PROGRAMMA

FRANZ SCHUBERT
1797-1828

***Ouverture, e kl. t.** (1819)

ROBERT SCHUMANN
1810-1856

Concert a kl. t., op. 54 (1841 en 1845)
VOOR PIANO EN ORKEST

Allegro affettuoso - Andante espressivo - Tempo primo - Allegro molto
Intermezzo: Andantino grazioso
Allegro vivace

Pauze

HENDRIK ANDRIESSEN
geb. 1892

Eerste symfonie (1930)

Lento - Allegro moderato, ma marcato
Andante tranquillo - Allegretto grazioso - Andante tranquillo
Allegro agitato

P. I. TSJAIKOWSKY
1840-1893

Romeo en Julia (1869)
OUVERTURE-FANTAISIE

ROYAL FESTIVAL HALL

GENERAL MANAGER: T. E. BEAN, C.B.E.

PHILHARMONIA CONCERT SOCIETY LTD

ARTISTIC DIRECTOR:

WALTER LEGGE

BEETHOVEN FESTIVAL

PHILHARMONIA ORCHESTRA

LEADER: HUGH BEAN

EDUARD VAN BEINUM

Overture, Prometheus, Op. 43

Symphony No. 4 in B flat, Op. 60

Symphony No. 5 in C minor, Op. 67

Sunday, 2nd November, 1958

at 7.30 p.m.

Programme One Shilling

IGOR STRAVINSKY (1882-1971)

Le chant du rossignol

Amsterdam 22 May 1956	COA	LP: Philips S 06130R LP: Epic LC 3274

L'oiseau de feu, suite

Amsterdam 6 April 1956	COA	LP: Philips S 06130R/6768 023

Le sacre du printemps

Amsterdam 11 September 1946	COA	78: Decca K 1727-1730/X 10166-10169 78: Decca (USA) EDA 59 CD: Beulah 2PD 11

PIOTR TCHAIKOVSKY (1840-1893)

Romeo and Juliet

London 12 January 1950	LPO	LP: Decca LXT 2531/ACL 11 LP: London LLP 167/LLP 376/LLP 737/ B 19027

Andante cantabile, arrangement

Amsterdam 22 September 1947	COA	78: Decca K 1871 78: London T 5365

Waltz (Serenade for strings)

Amsterdam 22 September 1947	COA	78: Decca K 1923/AK 1923

Casse noisette, suite

Amsterdam 30 April- 1 May 1958	COA	LP: Philips G 05342R/835 006AY/ ZKY 894 044 Valse des fleurs 45: Philips SBF 104

Casse noisette, Valse des fleurs

Amsterdam 22 September 1948	COA	78: Decca X 10165

Francesca da Rimini

London 12 November 1946	LPO	Decca unpublished

AMBROISE THOMAS (1811-1896)

Mignon, overture

Amsterdam 10 April 1956	COA	45: Philips NBE 11043/A402 063E LP: Philips GBL 5575/6768 023

JOHANN WAGENAAR (1862-1941)

The Taming of the Shrew, overture

Amsterdam 17-21 May 1943	COA	78: Polydor 68237

RICHARD WAGNER (1813-1883)

Lohengrin, Act 3 prelude

Amsterdam 20 September 1949	COA	78: Decca X 10256 78: Philips (Belgium) A 1113

Tannhäuser, overture and bacchanale

Amsterdam 20 September 1946	COA	Decca unpublished

CARL MARIA VON WEBER (1786-1826)

Euryanthe, overture

Amsterdam 21 September 1949	COA	78: Decca X 10191 May not have been published

Discographies

Teachers and pupils
Schwarzkopf / Ivogün / Cebotari /
Seinemeyer / Welitsch / Streich / Berger
7 separate discographies, 400 pages

The post-war German tradition
Kempe / Keilberth / Sawallisch /Kubelik /
Cluytens
5 separate discographies, 300 pages

Mid-century conductors
and More Viennese singers
Böhm / De Sabata / Knappertsbusch / Serafin /
Krauss / Dermota / Rysanek / Wächter /
Reining / Kunz
10 separate discographies, 420 pages

Leopold Stokowski
Discography and concert register, 300 pages

Tenors in a lyric tradition
Fritz Wunderlich / Walther Ludwig /
Peter Anders
3 separate discographies, 350 pages

Makers of the Philharmonia
Galliera / Susskind / Kletzki / Malko / Matacic /
Dobrowen / Kurtz / Fistoulari
8 separate discographies, 300 pages

A notable quartet
Janowitz / Ludwig / Gedda / Fischer-Dieskau
4 separate discographies, 600 pages

Hungarians in exile
Reiner / Dorati /Szell
3 separate discographies, 300 pages

The art of the diva
Muzio / Callas / Olivero
3 separate discographies, 225 pages

The lyric baritone
Reinmar / Hüsch / Metternich / Uhde /
Wächter
5 separate discographies, 225 pages

Price £22 per volume (£28 outside UK)
Special offer any 3 volumes for
£55 (£75 outside UK)
Postage included
Order from: John Hunt, Flat 6,
37 Chester Way, London SE11 4UR

Credits

Valuable help with the supply of information or illustration material for these discographies came from

Stathis Arfanis, Athens
Christopher Dyment, Welwyn
Richard Chlupaty, London
Clifford Elkin, Glasgow
Bill Flowers, London
Michael Gray, Alexandria VA
Syd Gray, Hove
Bill Holland, Polygram London
Ken Jagger, EMI Classics London
Raymond Klumper-Horneman, London
Roderick Krüsemann, Amsterdam
Johan Maarsingh, Utrecht
Nico Steffen, Huizen
Ronald Taylor, Barnet
Malcolm Walker, Harrow